My Cat Ate Aliens

and Other Humorous Tales in Veterinary Medicine

Natalie Griffin, D.V.M.

ISBN 978-1-64258-879-8 (paperback)
ISBN 978-1-64258-880-4 (digital)

Christian Faith Publishing, Inc.
832 Park Avenue
Meadville, PA 16335
www.christianfaithpublishing.com

A collection of unexpected, real-life stories from the world of veterinary medicine. They are fun, and we hope you enjoy.

Fiction based on true stories

Printed in the United States of America

To my mom, dad, husband,
and my four wonderful children who have supported me
throughout. I love you more than words can describe.

Introduction

Hello! Just to introduce myself, I am June B. French, veterinarian. I have wanted to be a veterinarian since I was five years old, when I began English horseback riding lessons. I never wanted to be anything else.

Oh yes, and I am also cheery, chatty, often gullible, positive, compassionate, and empathetic, and I scored an 8 out of 10 on a feeling-versus-practicality test. (Feelings won.) I have cried often for sad cases. I have rejoiced much in small victories. I am humored by sarcasm. So, that is me. Kind of a mess, but my husband likes it. Over the years, in order to deal with the many stressful days, I have filled a mental file cabinet with the craziness. The top-contending fun stories, especially the laugh-out-loud-crazy ones, are personal favorites. I am not funny and cannot tell jokes well, but the stories played out in front of me are often downright outrageous. They were head shakers, to say the least. They, along with some prayers, help brighten a challenging day. We must, of course, be serious and professional at work, but we can also laugh at what comes our way and try to enjoy the ride!

I changed all names in these stories to protect all involved, me included, because I feel I am not quite the same person today that I was in most of these rookie stories; but they are me, and my friends, and the stories are real. Here's to celebrating the fun and the funny and the challenges of veterinary medicine.

P.S. I also have a heart for rescue animals; they inspired me to write these stories. Please visit a shelter near you and take home your new best friend.

Contents

Decisions, Decisions

Kitty Mutt, clinic manager for a nonprofit animal shelter, sat at her desk, going about her hectic day. She was stressed over a difficult situation with a long-time donor. In place of her usual friendly smile, she wore a frown, and she could not help but let out a stressed sigh. This aloof benefactor was sticking her in a rotten position.

Managing the clinic for a rescue organization was a challenging job, and her days were often packed with managing volunteers, veterinarians, bills, rescue groups, financially destitute clients, and very odd situations. On Kitty Mutt's second day as manager, she'd encountered a loose giant pelican, which had casually strolled into her office and proceeded to squawk at her. She had quickly learned to respond to the craziness of animal welfare with patience and reason. Some days, however, were more challenging than others.

I, June B. French, DVM, was observing Kitty Mutt's obvious dilemma with empathy. A small-animal veterinarian by trade, I'd spent many joyful years volunteering with the shelter's adjoining low-cost clinic, and I'd had my own share of challenges that day.

Kitty sat near me in utter frustration while a longtime shelter donor made whimsical, unreasonable demands and threatened to pull her hefty annual donation. Kitty hung her head and massaged her brow. From my chair in the dark radiology room, where I sat typing information into the ultrasound machine, I could not help but become irritated too. I had sat through more than a few budget talks and knew what the loss of a $10,000 donation would mean.

"You did the right thing," I said uncertainly when she hung up the phone.

"I don't know what we're going to do if the money doesn't come through," Kitty said. "Some years, we get these large grants and donations, and then some years, we don't. There's no good way to predict it."

"Everyone works so hard, yet there's constant talk of decreased salaries and that sort of thing, It's so discouraging."

"He'll take care of us," I said. She acknowledged my meaning with a nod. Kitty and I had attended church together in the past, but sometimes, God's plan was hard to see.

The staff was driven so exceptionally hard to care for the saddest cases, to accommodate the most extreme financial straits. An average of three hundred animals per month were adopted out of the shelter—a massive achievement in the rescue arena. Our shelter even had a steady inflow of transfer patients from nearby shelters with low adoption rates. The shelter developed a low-cost veterinary clinic that serves low-income families. There was even a fund, aptly referred to as the Hope Fund, established to aid the extremely destitute clients, often elderly, who could not afford any medications for their animals. Recently, that fund had run dry. A large donation would ease some of the financial burden Kitty had to contend with now, but if the donor's demands were impossible to accommodate?

"Don't worry, it's better to do the right thing," I said.

Lord, it's so unfair. I wish I could reward the staff for doing the right thing, but I don't have that kind of money. I'm still buried in student loans, and with three kids to care for...

Just then, Shelly, a longtime vet assistant, walked in and presented me with my next ultrasound patient.

"This is Squeaks," she said. "She came from an animal hoarder with fifteen other flea-infested Pomeranians. She appears to be about five years old."

The five-pound pooch looked up at me with sweet eyes. She had a speckled coloring called blue merle, multicolored irises in both eyes, and her hair extended out in the most beautiful fluff.

"Oh. What's wrong?"

"Well, she came in with a large group of dogs, but she's the only one that is heartworm[1] positive, and her chest X-rays look bad. Really bad," Shelly said.

"Okay," I said. "So, I'm supposed to ultrasound her, and?"

"Well," Shelly replied, "we're pretty much leaving it up to you to decide if this one should be treated or euthanized."

"Well that…is *horrible*."

A somber Shelly nodded. I'm certain she could see how wonderful Squeaks's little personality was, but unfortunately, Shelly and I had both seen advanced illnesses plenty of times before. We knew what sort of complications we would risk if we opted for treatment.

Squeaks looked up at me with her sweet, tiny face.

"Yeah, it sucks," Shelly said calmly. "The shelter manager is leaving it up to you."

Great.

I picked up the ultrasound probe to examine the Pomeranian's heart. Unfortunately, it was chockful of heartworms. They were consuming the entire right side of her heart. I sighed.

Should I give her a chance? Should I spare her the agony of an intense treatment protocol, one she may not live through?

Squeaks peered up at me. *Save her. Save her for sure. But she's so small. So small. We have to try, right?*

My mind was racing. Shelly was staring at Squeaks with the utmost compassion and gently stroking the Pomeranian's fluff. She recognized the firestorm in my brain. It's like staring down a necessary tunnel, but it is dark and you are not sure where it will lead, but hope pulls you into it.

---

[1] *Heartworm disease is a parasitic, mosquito-borne disease in which long worms take up residence in the right side of the heart and pulmonary arteries of its victims, primarily dogs. It easily can be prevented. If contracted and allowed to progress, it eventually will cause heart failure and death. Heartworm disease has four grades that veterinarians use to try to determine treatment protocols if the animal is heartworm positive. Grade 1 is a minimal infection, with no changes to heart and lungs; grade 4 is severe infection with a high worm "burden," or count, and with cardiac, pulmonary, and liver involvement.*

At this point, I labeled "Squeaks" as a grade 3 heartworm infection.

Lord, what to do for Squeaks? What to do for Kitty Mutt? There are so many animals to treat…I just don't know.

A short while later, the receptionist at the front of the shelter clinic called back to Kitty's office.

"Kitty?" she said. "There's a woman on the phone who says her CAT ATE ALIENS."

"What? You sure?" said Kitty.

"Oh yes, I asked twice. She's quite certain."

"Well, that's nice," Kitty said in a sarcastic tone that implied she was not surprised, given that craziness was a daily routine. "All right, I'll deal with it."

Shutting the donor problems out of her thoughts, Kitty calmly picked up the phone and said in a bright voice, "Ma'am, hello?"

The Eagle

I had just started rotations at the vet school's small animal clinic and, after three long, hard years of intense studying, was super excited and full of anticipation. We got to go to the "hands-on" part of our four-year journey through vet school. I was currently on small-animal orthopedics, a rotation specializing in surgeries for bone- and tendon-related problems. I had a clinical professor, Dr. English, who was a bit proud and well versed. He knew his surgical stuff, had arrogant humor, and sneered at students a bit. He was nice overall, and I was thankful for his teaching, but he expected you to be serious. He liked every *t* crossed and every *i* dotted, so to speak. He would grill you with questions and expect you to be prepared with clinically applicable knowledge at all times. He would snicker when you fell into his quiz traps. For me, this was extremely discouraging. Dr. English always seemed moderately amused in exposing weakness. As vet students, we still had to earn grades in clinical rotations based on our knowledge, attitude, and performance.

There is a general routine in the mornings at vet school for fourth year students. Usually, first thing, you address your cases in the hospital and touch base with clinicians and residents. Then you are off to the only class of the day at 8:00 a.m. Often, you try to get some coffee and a bagel at the bagel shop before class. At 9:00 a.m., you rejoin your rotation. You meet in the rounding rooms with a resident and the lead clinician. You review the cases coming in that day. Everyone picks a case that interests them. Throughout the day, you meet with the owner, examine the pet, and review a case plan. This is where the clinician turns to you and starts picking your brain about what you would do and then guides you to what's best. Then you help get lab tests, take animals to radiology, turn in any requests to pharmacy, etc. It is very busy, but fun and exciting most days.

One sunny day, several days into the small-animal orthopedics rotation, I went about my morning and made it to the meeting room where we do rounds. Somehow, there was a case on the board that made my jaw drop. Being polite, I looked at the three other students and noticed they had put their names next to the other cases. (What? Are you crazy?). I felt it was a great rarity, an *eagle* on the small-animal orthopedics rotation, one overseen by the university. In fact, this particular patient was none other than Auburn University's War Eagle, who flies across the football field during games.

Seriously, I was drooling, even though I'm not really that into birds. I once again asked if the others were all sure they did not want this case. They all just said, "You go ahead." I was so thrilled; I was literally jumping up and down with a permanent grin on my face. Dr. English sneered and chortled, "It's not that big of a deal." To which I responded, "Oh yes, it is! I am so excited!"

"Okay, it's your case," he said, shaking his head, and obviously thinking, *Ridiculous vet students.*

Initially, while I was on small-animal clinics, we did not get a lot of exotics or any animals other than the usual lineup—dogs and cats. I remember one of the interns early on nursing a pigeon back to health, and everyone asking her about it all the time; her pigeon was considered our exotic. Later in the year, however, with a 450-pound tiger, a 3,000-pound bull, and a zebra foal, I would change my mind on my "exotics" experience. But for now, I saw this eagle as a totally unique opportunity, and I was pumped. We did have a raptor rehabilitation center nearby, but I had rarely seen the cases.

I patiently but eagerly awaited my turn to receive my patient. The other students casually took on their cases. Then it was my turn; the 10:00 a.m. appointment arrived, and there she was. The eagle came in for treatment of a foot condition called Bumblefoot. She was beautiful and enormous. I was more nervous than around the largest horse. Her condition is actually a fairly common condition for the birds who are in captivity. Her foot had been bandaged and treated. She was coming in for a recheck.

So, there I was. A vet school medical photographer showed up and took a photo. My patient had a handler wearing a special glove holding her. My super stern professor asked me to remove the bandages; I looked up at the handler, who could probably tell I was a novice. He laid the eagle on his long arm, her back against his glove and her belly and claws facing up. She was perfectly still, like a statue, a reflection of her advanced training.

I carefully started to remove the bandages one at a time. Dr. English looked at me with a grimace. Then he showed me, using his own hand as an example, how to manually pull apart the claws and check under her foot. "Be careful," he said in his gruff serious tone.

"Uh, oh yes, sir," I said.

Slow and steady. I had never been this close to one of these birds before. Slowly, I grasped her huge talons, or claws. She didn't seem to mind. Carefully, with everyone watching, I began opening the talons up to check the bottom side of her foot. As the talons opened up, the foot made the most horrible creaking noise. It was like her bones were crumpling and grinding against each other. I panicked, gasped.

Dr. English jumped forward and yelled, "Oh no! You BROKE her!"

My mouth dropped; I jumped back; I slapped my hands over my mouth. I had been so careful. I had been so excited about this case, and now I had broken this beautiful bird. My stomach dropped. *Completely crushed, trying to make sense...*

"Ha-ha!" he said. "Just kidding! I got you! Their feet always make that creaky noise." Dr. English continued to laugh and snort at me.

*Insert, totally just got played.

(Shaking Head)

Actually, not that funny at the time.

I had a blank stare for one long minute.

I bandaged her feet after all had been inspected and addressed. I carried my fallen joyous self out of the exam room. I glared at my professor who made me believe I had broken the BELOVED Auburn mascot. He looked at me, amused, victorious in his crappy joke capabilities. Oh well, at least I got a photo.

The eagle finally made it out of her bandages a few weeks later when I was off the orthopedics rotation. I jogged past her atrium on the university grounds, and she sat perched high with nothing on her feet. I smiled at her; she was a good patient, and I was relieved, she had not been broken.

In 2014, fifteen years after my encounter, at the age of thirty-four, this eagle took her last flight and died in the halls of our vet school, cherished and not forgotten. This story is to honor her for her beautiful service and recognize the Raptor Rehabilitation program at Auburn University.

An Electrifying Morning

I was a bit prissy in vet school about some things. I had a lot of large-animal experience, but it was all limited to horses, having spent my childhood at horse shows and equestrian events. I was an avid pony clubber and a three-day eventer. I loved dressage. Did I know horses? Yes. Horses were my inspiration; they got me to vet school. Somehow that gave me some unknown and sorely misplaced large animal medicine confidence around all the cowboys and cowgirls that were in my vet school class. However, I was not raised on a farm. The truth is, I had not really played on farms, only in stables, and there's a difference. So here is a simple lesson: Horses are not cows.

At my vet school, we were a bit old school. They believe—and I loved this—in experiencing all major aspects of veterinary medicine and learning it all. Hands on. That is, cows, horses, dogs, cats, goats, sheep, and small mammals, regardless of your personal interests.

In senior year of veterinary college, you are required to do a rotation in every aspect of veterinary medicine. One of these rotations for large-animal medicine includes a rotation on dairy. I was having fun experiencing this difficult *4:00 a.m.* chore. You just roll out of bed, put your coveralls on, and head to the vet school large-animal clinic in the wee hours. The cows were lined up, ready to be milked, mobbing the gateway, super anxious to get in. I'm not sure if it's the pressure of a full udder, the need for breakfast or perhaps just the never-ending routine, or all of these factors.

The vet school was always quiet and dark at these hours, which was a nice change from the very busy hustle of activity during the day. In the early morning, the facilities always appeared clean, and there was a quietness that was somewhat soothing. All the smells of being on a farm and the cool air of the morning. It took my imagi-

17

nation to what it must be like to experience and to love the peace of just you and the animals on a real farm in the early morning.

We were required to milk just about every morning for two weeks. We learned about the pipelines and the quality of the milk. We also learned about "teat care"—very important, since it is yielding a product that is in high demand for human consumption. Quality had to be high. We even were taught about different teats, and one cow had an extra, fifth teat.

My dairy professor was a stout, body-building cowboy type. We'll call him Dr. Tough. He unfortunately had to look after five female vet students, all routed in small-animal medicine and in equine. Thank you, sir, that we were never hurt, even though we tortured you daily by making up songs every morning to the beat of the milking machines and giggled endlessly.

One day, our dairy professor, Dr. Tough, asked for a volunteer. It was 5:00 a.m., and I was tired and very hungry. I raised my hand, I don't know why; maybe it was because we couldn't think up any more songs, but he picked me. He asked if I could go up on the hill to a certain pasture and check on the heifers (female cows) to see if any looked like they could be in heat. "Okay," I said, believing that all the cow in heat does is irritate the other cows to express this hormonal activity. So off I went to check the cows; seems easy enough. By myself, in this case, thank goodness.

So my familiarity was misplaced for being knowledgeable in large-animal life, and on this particular morning, it would definitely disservice me. In the land of horses, in pastures, in riding rings, etc., often to keep horses off the fence and to keep them from destroying it, the top wire is hot, electric. It will shock you. I have accidentally run into it before while taking care of my pony as a kid. It stings, really bad. I knew this, twenty years' worth of being aware, the top wire is hot.

I walked past the treatment barns and up a hill about a half mile from the dairy barn. No one was around. The sun was beginning to peak, so there was a good bit of morning light.

I approached the fence to the cows with my overconfident self. There was a large, peaceful herd grazing, slowly moving about. The gate was a ways off, like twenty feet, much too far. I just sighed and decided it was quicker to go through the fence.

This particular fence was five wires high, with a post about every eight feet, but I knew not to go near the top wire. What I didn't know, however, was that cows can do things horses can't. I grabbed two wires in the middle of the fence, pulled them apart in a quarter of second, and started to jump through.

In midair, a gigantic pulse of what seemed like lightning went through me—through my arms, across my heart, and throughout my WHOLE body. Yes, it zapped, buzzed, electrified, and stunned me. To this day, I believe I got frozen. In midair. With electric current buzzing throughout my arms and across my chest—an image that probably belongs in a comic strip—finally, I hit the other side of the fence, and I let go. I had screamed absolutely horribly loud, much like a shrieking cat. I lay there in the grass, stunned, muscles frozen, staring at the sky. I could not believe it; I had assumed that only the top was electric. I was thankful some of my fellow competitive, eager-to-poke fun vet students were not around to witness such a display in LACK of basic knowledge. That's when I realized I was actually not alone.

There were so many eyes on me, it was unnerving. As I sat up, they all stared without blinking. None of these eyes were human. For some reason, it was equally embarrassing. I had awoken a herd of dairy cows that had been eating and grazing and going about their day. Now I was their focus. There were at least forty cows, and none moved or chewed or shook their heads; they just stared right at me. I bet that they were all having a good chuckle to themselves at the ridiculous vet student who did not know all the wires were hot. I stared back, humiliated.

All the cows knew.

Yes, I did it. Make fun of me later, will you. I got up and wandered around, dizzy and sick and not well enough to go back. I tripped on some grass and fell—again.

The cows eventually went back to grazing. I watched them. Some of them seemed hyperactive. I wrote the tag numbers down.

"Where were you?" Dr. Tough asked when I returned.

"Oh, I just watched for a while." I gave him the tag numbers of the agitated cows, and he confirmed that those were the cows he had suspected would be in heat. I was a tad relieved that maybe I had done this part of my assigned task correctly.

"Hey, are you okay?" he said, giving me a serious look.

"Oh yes, fine thanks."

"All right," he said, definitely not sure of my response. I finished my tasks and went on to 8:00 a.m. class. I told myself that maybe I should check a mirror or something. But instead, I grabbed a bagel at the coffee shop and ran to class.

I sat in class. I felt terrible. I was staring at my coffee and bagel, hoping they would revive me somehow. It was not happening for me. A classmate I didn't often chat with came walking over to me from the far side of the room. She asked, "Are you okay?"

"Uh yes, fine," I said. She stared at me for a moment, concerned, then politely walked away. I sat there thinking the exchange was odd.

Then two of my best friends who were sitting in front of me. Hannah Pom and Cassie Corgi turned around and glared at me.

"Are you okay?" Hannah asked. She tended to be sweet but frank.

"Yeah, sure," I said, trying to convince her.

She was unimpressed, and because she was a good friend, said boldly:

"Well, you look REALLY awful."

Oh dear. What do you say? I made a stupid mistake and electrocuted myself? I just said nothing. Later, I found a mirror. My hair was zapped crazy with little broken blond ends going every which way, and I had horrible black circles under my eyes. Lovely.

It was many years before I shared this story. Cow folks know a cow can sneak through a fence.

In Rut

In rut—it's a phrase used to describe a male goat having seasonal hormonal activity. I was in my third year of vet school when I learned this. Now, I had no experience with goats or sheep, or anything of that kind. We were learning all about their various cycles, behaviors, illnesses, nutrition, and diseases. But I thought it was so odd that a male goat would have a testosterone cycle. Odd. When in that cycle, they display all sorts of inappropriate behavior, trying to get the attention of a female who is also in season. Makes sense, I guess.

In vet school, this term is used on and off jokingly, as you can imagine, because vet school, excluding the nice married people, was a lot like high school in social aspects.

But anyway, educated about goats, I finished my final exams for the quarter and went home for break.

Here's one thing I would like to tell everyone. I am a runner. I ran cross country in high school, and I never stopped. I have never been particularly fast, but I have finished many a race, including the New York City marathon, twice.

My parents, always supportive of my love of horses, lived in a suburb close to some land so they could have one or two horses on our property. It was wonderful. They had moved there in my second year of high school.

When I went running in these parts, my parents' beloved pup, Stewart, would always come with me. He was a streetwise bird dog and loved to run, dipping in and out of all the various smells in the side bushes and fields. In the country, running is nice, but it's also a little awkward if there are not a lot of people around, or if a loose dog notices you.

I was feeling emotional and moody one day, so I decided to go out for a run. I went extra far that day, but for whatever reason, Stewart was not with me. Somehow, I ended way out in Farmville, USA.

That's when I realized I had a follower. It was a goat. He was loose on the side of the road. *Hmm.* I didn't know whose he was. I had never seen a goat before. He had big horns, I can tell you that. Oh, and he was acting very strange.

I started to run away just to ignore him, but then I looked over my shoulder and there he was again, trotting fifteen feet behind me. I stopped and tried to shoo him away. I guess I gave him some mixed signals because he started to do the most inappropriate licking of himself, specifically his male body parts. Then he urinated. Yuck, goat.

"Go away! GO!"

Then I realized, *Oh my! Just like they had described, this thing is "in rut." But what is going on…**I appear to be the target**!*

"GOOO AWAAAY!"

I ran faster. He followed. I tried to shoo him—no luck. It still showed me, clearly, he was misinterpreting my signals. He stuck his top lip in the air and curled it back, a clear sign: in rut.

Ewwww. Gross.

I ran faster with purpose and fear, but he kept up.

AHHHHH! This went on for two miles or more. My heart was pounding.

So creepy and it's just not right…

(Note: This is before everyone had cell phones.)

Eventually, I was running hard, not jogging at all. My lungs started burning, but the goat wasn't fazed at all. He effortlessly was keeping up.

I finally saw a car coming. My longtime next-door neighbor. Relief! I waved frantically. He stopped.

"Can you take me home?"

"Uh, sure. You okay?"

"Noooooooooo. That goat is chasing me!"

He glanced at the goat. He chuckled and drove me home. He had been a family friend and a farmer type for a long time. He looked at me awkwardly, like he knew what might've set the goat off.

"Yeah," he said very slowly. "Mmmhmm, sometimes they do that to the ladies."

Farm girls would tell me much later that goats go nuts when humans are experiencing "the monthly friend."

Well, they did not mention it in class.

The Professor Who Drank Sweet Tea

Senior year of vet school, I, being a horse enthusiast and small-animal-based student, was excited to go on a special rotation called large-animal ambulatory. This is where we ride in a vet truck and go out to all the surrounding farms and attempt to perform large-animal services with proficiency and skill. It was also a fun chance to get out during the day, away from the school, a refreshing change from the halls that were part of our world 24/7 for four years.

This rotation employed two of the most well-liked, fun, and respected professors of the entire university staff to oversee our attempts at being doctors. One was Dr. Ginny Steer, a tough, no-frills-type veterinarian. She once taught my entire class how to file fine edges that develop on an equine's teeth, a procedure known as "floating." Ninety students looked on while she lectured, reviewed, and then sedated and floated an adult horse. Also, she was eight and a half months pregnant and barely broke a sweat, just spoke fast and had to take deep breaths from time to time. wow. Then there was the other professor, Dr. Al D. Paca, greatly loved and well known for countless crazy lectures, full of unimaginable enthusiasm, and endless, side-splitting stories. Dr. Al D. Paca, a professor who loves sweet tea.

Here I was again with five other students on my rotation, and none of them were guys. We did have a fifty-fifty male-female ratio in my class. But for whatever luck, it was five girls, one of whom was pregnant, in the care of Dr. Paca for most of the rotation. He was a Deep South professor, and he had had a lot of experience in private practice and specialty practice and has multiple letters after his name. He was a board-certified large-animal theriogenologist and a board-certified nutritionist. He was big on being a dad and a devoted husband. He loved the Bible and only wore Dickies cov-

24

eralls. In addition, he was proud to be the next-door-neighbor type and always wanted his clients to call him by his first name only. His unimaginable tales lit a spark in me to embrace the crazy, so you can chuckle later.

He told us one tale that has never left me, and which I have retold often. It was an inconceivable tale of starfish extract. At the root of his crazy stories, I found an amazing tool to help with what was to come: finding the humor—a helpful resource for dealing with the daily surplus of overwhelming and improbable situations.

Every morning, Dr. Paca would stop at the nearby drive-through barbecue house before our day began and order himself a large sweet tea. The barbecue house always seemed to recognize the rumble of Dr. Paca's big diesel engine. When he ordered sweet tea, the standard response was, "You got it, boss."

On day one of ambulatory, we all piled into the truck and drove to a nearby dairy farm where there was a sick cow. We all had our side pouches with thermometers and army knives—professional looking with clean matching scrub tops and stethoscopes around our necks. Very professional; we just needed the knowledge part to sink in a bit more.

We looked at all the milking equipment while walking with the dairy managers. We began our history taking. We asked about the febrile animal's previous care. The caretakers had already treated her with many routine medications for teat infection, and nothing seemed to be working. This cow was also known to be a "high producer," a valuable cow.

Five students and one professor examined the cow in question. We found her to be very dehydrated and with a mild fever. Dr. Paca said he was concerned and that we should send her to the vet school for care and diagnostics, especially since we were only two miles up the road. "But first," he said, "we should hydrate her. So, how much fluid would it take to hydrate this cow, children?"

We all calculated with our pocket calculators for a four-hundred-kilogram bovine, 8–10 percent dehydrated. Several five-liter fluid bags would be appropriate, probably twenty liters at least.

"Does anyone know a fast way to get twenty liters of fluid in that cow before she goes to the clinic?" he asked, with a gleam in his eye and a trick in his pocket.

Five vet students shook their heads.

"Can't she just get hooked up to fluids when she gets there?' I asked.

"Nah, not necessary."

He quizzed us some more. No answers. Then he went out to his truck and grabbed a one-liter bottle of hypertonic saline. He said, "Give this, and what will happen?" We started to answer eagerly—"Will pull fluid from extracellular places, blah-blah-blah—medical term, medical term, physiologic process—blah-blah-blah."

"And what else?" said Dr. Paca, dismayed.

No answer.

"If I gave you a bunch of salt, what would you do?"

We all looked around at each other, hoping someone would know the answer.

Uncomfortable silence…

"Drink?" finally one person said. (It was not me, but I was thankful).

"Yes," he smiled.

He then proceeded to hook up the cow and gave her this seemingly small bottle of fluid through a large-gauge needle.

"How will that ever be enough?" I asked.

"Oh, it will," he said.

Into the jugular vein the saline went. It only took a few minutes.

The cow was tied next to a water trough, but due to the tie, she could only move her head a little.

So when the little bottle ran dry, he detached the cow from the IV line and then untied the rope. The cow stormed straight for the giant water trough as if she had a desperate mission, a mission for water. She plunged her head and, gulp after gulp after gulp, she drained it. Once or twice, she stopped for just a moment, to breathe, but then she would plunge again and continue. There before us, in the span of five minutes, this bovine consumed approximately at least twenty liters of water, and the trough was almost empty.

"Whelp, that'll do," Dr. Paca said, smiling.

Later, a call with an update on her condition came in from the vet school. The cow was getting treatment, and despite her illness, she was surprisingly very well hydrated.

We dealt with sheep, llamas, and cattle; but mostly we saw horses that were pregnant or needing to be bred. We castrated a few calves. We met a few owners who were "Deep South" and a few lady horse owners who were particularly "sassy."

On the fourth day, we seemed to be losing our top-student collectiveness, if we ever had it. We lost some blood tubes for Coggins test, important for horse travel (me). Then we broke some hormone medication bottles at a reproduction call. Dr. Paca kept saying, "That's all right, be okay."

Finally, we headed out to an aloof owner who wanted to know if her mare was ovulating.

We pulled onto her property, a beautiful farm with warm-blood horses running in the pasture. Dr. Paca said that since we were on a bit of a streak of fumbling, maybe we could try to pull it together. He informed us, "This client complains a lot. She's quite prissy."

So we all got out and were introduced. We had tidied up. She confirmed that she indeed had a mare for breeding and wanted to ultrasound her ovaries to see if she was close to ovulation. No problem, said Dr. Paca. She glared at all the students like we were subacceptable entities that she had to deal with. She turned toward the barn to get her horse. Dr. Paca told me since I had an interest in equine medicine, I would be able to ultrasound.

No problem! I said, so excited. *Ultrasound is my favorite!*

I ran over to the box with the ultrasound and pulled it off the truck. That's when it slipped out of my hands and hit the asphalt.

Dr. Paca gasped (portable ultrasounds cost usually about $20,000—at least)

In a panic, I picked it up. Much to my dismay, the front screen popped off the machine and hit the dirt.

Dr. Paca looked like he wanted to cry; he opened his mouth to yell, but no words came out.

My best bud, Cassie Corgi, took the screen out of the dirt, blew the dirt off with her mouth, and popped it back on the machine. It clicked into place. Dr. Paca still looked tearful. Everybody stood silently. Another vet school pal, Amy, looked cautiously at Paca then slowly reached for the power button. We all held our breath. I said a silent prayer; the screen came to life, a perfect sonogram image. Whew.

Without any more words, we all walked steadily into Miss Prissy-Pants' fancy horse barn and, like total experts, identified that her mare had a follicle on her ovary and was in her time frame for needing to be bred. Total experts.

And that's how many of the vet calls with Dr. Paca were never dull, but full of emotion and unforeseen drama. Dr. Paca loved it. But one day, one of my friends put a look of fear on him. She gave him a tale that he still to this day has not recovered from. It was a new adventure that evidently he had not been dealt with before.

My longtime pal Cassie, a country girl from Kentucky with a thick country accent, happened to be on this rotation with us. She had loads of large-animal experience from back home in Kentucky. However, at this point, she was also seven months pregnant. Not the most ideal scenario, but she always, always made the best of it. She worked hard and tried not to ever complain, but one day, she let one little pregnant complaint escape her lips, and Dr. Paca went into a state of panic.

We were at a farm vaccinating cows. Cassie was taking down their numbers, doing the paperwork for each cow that was vaccinated. All the cows have tags that are located on their ears. I was sticking the cows with the vaccines in one pen, and another of my vet pals was vaccinating in another pen. There was a lot of chaos. Dr. Paca hollered that he had run out of vaccines. He was also trying to help the cow into the isolated stocks. He seemed to be a particularly crafty cow, not willing at all to get his shots. Cassie picked up some extra vaccines, ran over, and stuck the shot in the cow's neck. The cow jumped, and she jumped back. She was never in the way of his legs since he can't kick at her through his stocks.

Dr. Paca looked up said, "Thanks," but quickly glanced back at her. Cassie Corgi was holding her side with her hand.

"You all right?" he asked, his eyes wide and serious. We all glanced over at seven-months-pregnant Cassie.

"Yeah, I guess," she chuckled. "I think I might've strained my uterus."

"You did what?!" Dr. Paca was in an instant panic. He ran over to her.

"Do you want me to take you to the hospital?" (Dr. Paca had the overpowering "daddy" concerned look.)

"No, I'll be all right," Cassie Corgi said with her quiet stoicism.

Dr. Paca looked scared, unnerved. He gave Cassie a solid eyeball glare with vessels popping out of his bald head. He finished up vaccinating the last few cattle, and we all piled into the vet truck. He helped Cassie Corgi into the front-seat passenger side. She was still holding her side.

She started to breathe deeply.

"Oh Lord, help us!" cried Dr. Paca.

Cassie looked at him and tried to calm him down. "It's really not that bad. I think I'll be fine."

All of us were worried about her now.

"You're going to the doctor," stated Dr. Paca.

"No, I'm fine."

"Maybe we should take you back to the equine treatment area and ultrasound you," I said. It is easy to see a baby on the machines and relatively easy to find the heartbeat, plus I love ultrasound. (Us mommy vets are guilty of checking it often at our clinics.)

Dr. Paca seemed happy with this. He turned the truck sharply and started driving toward the vet school.

"No, really, I'm fine," Cassie protested. "It's not that bad. I think you guys are overreacting."

Dr. Paca looked at Cassie Corgi, "You are in my care, and you said YOU STRAINED YOUR UTERUS!"

"Yeah, well, I think I did," she chuckled.

"Ugh," said Dr. Paca, totally irritated at her attitude toward her condition.

Now we were all looking on as the two of them a started to duke it out in a verbal fight. Dr. Paca, despite being a theriogenologist, which is like an OB-GYN for large animals, was not wanting to be responsible for a human with a strained uterus whatsoever. He was probably having every uterine problem he teaches us about crash through his brain. Being a renowned expert on reproduction, he was silently, uncontrollably, applying his great knowledge on uteruses to Cassie's current side stitch. All of this was adding to an epic level of stress within the great mind of Dr. Paca. Cassie Corgi, who is a stubborn workhorse, stood her ground that she did not want any special attention.

However, she kept rubbing her side and occasionally would let out a deep breath. Dr. Paca drove faster. We pulled into the vet school. There were five trailers outside of the equine treatment room and piles of people.

"I am not going in there, there's a mess of people in there, and besides, I am fine. It's just a bit of a cramp. Maybe I should just lie down for a few," Cassie said, finally conceding a little.

"Let's take her in the bovine treatment area and put her on the hydraulic table," said one of our fellow rotation students. "She can rest there, and then you can stick the ultrasound on her, Dr. Paca,"

A bovine hydraulic table is a huge table built to withstand up to three-thousand-pound bulls. You attach the bull or cow to one side and strap in his neck and his feet. It is matted on the one side where the cow is, to make it nice for the animal. The table, with huge hydraulic force, slowly turns the cow to a horizontal position. This is most often used so that veterinarians can work on cow hooves.

All the other vet students chimed in, "Yeah that's an idea. It'll be more confined and private in the bovine room."

"Cassie, you'll be comfortable," I said.

"You are not putting me on the hydraulic table! I want no part of that!"

Years later, I would understand, no pregnant woman ever wants to be associated with being or looking like a cow, or in this case, actually potentially requiring a cow's exam table.

"You should go to the doctor, a HUMAN doctor, then, for a strained uterus," Dr. Paca pled.

"No, I am fine!"

"Well, I have never had such a problem all my years of being a professor, but I don't want to be the one to deliver your baby."

Cassie conceded to calling her doctor, who told her just to go home and rest, which she did. She took some Tylenol. She came back the next day with no problems. Her baby wasn't delivered until forty-two weeks of pregnancy, or two weeks past the due date: a healthy boy. However, Dr. Paca never forgot the episode of the strained uterus and has embellished this story ever since.

In the days that followed, as we rode around with Dr. Paca, we started noticing a couple of oddities: first, Dr. Paca would never stop to go to the restroom; and second, farm dogs liked to mark our vet truck, even when there seemed to be no farm dogs around. We had complained on occasion about the lack of bathroom visits—we were five girls after all, one pregnant. He would shrug his shoulders and say in his Southern drawl, "Sure, just let me know and I'll stop." Cassie even commented on how much sweet tea Dr. Paca drank. "You don't have to go?" Bit of a mystery, it was.

It was me, unfortunately, who busted my esteemed professor on this mystery in the most inopportune fashion.

We went to a farm to check on a horse with a laceration. As I recall, it wasn't terrible, but it needed care and bandaging. Now when we came up to a farm, usually the professor would assess the situation and would review with us what to do. He often would quiz us. Vet students are usually ready and willing to get their hands-on experience and prove their knowledge. We sometimes selected a lead person. For this case, we needed a holder, a wound scrubber, and someone to go over the estimate with owner. These were all routine assignments. I believe I was asked to help the wound care scrubber and be a bandage person. Being a horse show girl, I like bandaging and wrapping horse legs. The wound scrubber was wearing gloves, and I was handing materials. The horse was inside the pasture fence as we were treating it. There was a big gate that the vet truck was parked next to, and the horse was standing just on the other side of the fence from the vet truck, near the gate. This becomes important.

At one point, I was asked by the wound scrubber to go back to the vet truck and get some additional wound-scrubbing supplies.

Little did I know that my professor was carefully watching the gate to see if any vet students came through. He didn't see any. I decided that even though the gate was only ten feet from me, it was quicker just to go **under** the fence. So I did. Well, that's when I ran up on my poor professor, *voiding* on the vet truck tire.

He was shell shocked. He zipped up his Dickies is a rush and immediately began fussing at me. "What are you doing? Why didn't you use the gate? Ah, crap…"

He now had wet Dickies. Oh my, I was in for it. I apologized profusely. I ran back to the horse and bandaged its leg. We left that call, and he was a bit silent, but just for a moment. Then he proceeded to vent to all my fellow vet students in the truck about what I had done and now, in addition, he was most uncomfortably wet. He was upset, shaking his head, but you could see the humor in the story building behind his smirk. He was fussing, but his round cheeks and bald head were full of humor.

"Because of her, I wet myself." Dr. Paca took a deep breath and smiled. "Guess we need to make a pit stop at the vet school."

He loved students for the senseless happenings that only go with students and farm calls.

For the record, I never saw anything but a man standing next to a truck and a wet tire. He shook his head multiple times and banged on the steering wheel, "June, why didn't you just use the gate?" Now everyone, but me, was shaking all over with chuckles. One of my friends saved me. "Well, now we know why he never has to stop to go to the bathroom."

Target Practice Needed

Prior to vet school, I worked for five years in a small-animal clinic in my hometown. These local veterinarians, some of them alumni from my school, were excellent mentors and tried every day I was there to explain the ins and outs of veterinary medicine. I was trained in all the routine stuff: medications, nail trims, surgery prep, blood work, temperature checks, etc. I was proficient at most basic stuff in a small-animal hospital prior to going to vet school. I regularly performed a common veterinary procedure called anal gland expression.

Now, these glands are not the prettiest of topics. Anal glands are two scent glands located next to the rectum in dogs and cats. They have small sacs full of liquid material and a duct that sends the material out on to stool. This gland is most commonly stimulated to "express" the fluid out by territorial behaviors or fearful situations. However, domestication of our pets allows them to settle for a life of safe walks, routine meals, couches, and minimal interactions with lions and tigers and that sort of thing. Some pets don't have any problems with their glands, but many do. The glands will fill full of a malodorous material that makes the pets itch, lick, and scoot their bottoms horribly across carpets. This devastates most owners. It is a simple procedure to express the glands. In most pets, it takes only a few minutes and two gentle squeezes. The pets are greatly relieved, and so are the owners.

One day in vet school, we were in a wet lab (hands-on work-shop) called small-animal diagnostics. It's where students do all the routine procedures and review normal physical exams. Clinicians make sure students can draw blood, collect urine, and review normal things like "reverse sneezing," a common presentation in dogs. Our group consisted of four people—me and three very nice small-animal folks whom I had also had my small animal surgery wet labs with. In small-animal surgery, we spayed and neutered shelter animals. In small-animal diagnostics, our professors brought in a large group of small dogs, beagles mostly.

One of my GOOD friends, Bonnie Falcon, was in my group. She had interests outside of small animal; she also liked bird and rabbit medicine. She was of small stature—five feet max—and had straight blond hair. She was nice and fun but often quiet and serious. The two other group members would go on to work with small animals after graduation; one is a fellow working mommy with three sons and the other is a military veterinarian. Thank you, sir, for your service—you know who you are.

So we were all together in small-animal diagnostic class one day, and it was time to go over anal glands. Yes, those two little glands in the back end of a dog that cause clients so much grief.

None of the others in my group had done this before. I told them just to go ahead because I had done it many times, for years, in fact. They decided that I should be the one to express the glands and demonstrate how it is done.

"Are you sure?" I asked.

Yes, they all said. Bonnie said she would really prefer to be shown first.

Well, all right. I felt a little proud to already be proficient in something. Plus, this was a simple-enough task.

Sure, I'll do it and show you guys.

The beagle wagged his tail happily.

My fellow group members asked me a few questions about technique. Well, I explained, it was just like squeezing a grape or a raisin, at about four o'clock and eight o'clock on the rectum. Gross, I know, but it is a source of much frustration; and we, the veterinarians, have to be able to respond.

It's really simple, but it smells awful.

I mean, the rotting fish smell is actually really terrible. Really. It is terribly pungent and is known to linger. You have to try to make sure that it is completely cleaned off the pet afterwards and that none of it gets near you while you are doing it. Bonnie was looking on in a serious nature over my shoulder. Trevor, who was rather tall, was standing behind me, and Betsy was on my other side.

I went for it.

Glove on, paper towel ready to catch the dreadful material that came out. Eager puppy with tail up. I remember grabbing the gland on the left first. Instead of a grape size, it was more like a large plum. I started to squeeze, but it was requiring a bit of pressure. Maybe it was clogged; I was unsure. Everyone was staring, and I was demonstrating. I said I knew what was I was doing, but nothing was happening.

"Do you want us to get a clinician?" said Trevor, concerned.

For anal glands, the easiest thing at the clinic? UGH!

"No," I said, with my little stint of pride that destroyed me moments later.

So I pushed the towel down and looked a little. Nothing looked odd in appearance, so I decided I would just squeeze harder.

That worked.

It shot up, out, and over my shoulder like a rocket, a fire hose of rotten fluid.

I turned around to my left. Hoping it wasn't true.

But it was.

There was Bonnie, utterly disgusted; it had hit her on the forehead, and it was dripping down her sweet face and over her little cheeks.

"June, I'm gonna [expletive] you."

"Uhhh…" I choked on my humiliation, "I'm so sorry. I had the towel, I don't know what happened. SORRY."

I tried to get her a towel. She wiped her face. The smell was awful. Really, really awful.

I fussed over her for some time; everyone was smiling and cringing at the same time.

"Sorry, sorry, I'm so sorry…"

"Just get on with it!" she yelled.

And so…I did.

*Happy to report that, somehow, we are still friends (although now only through social media). ☺

An Unusual Affair

Wile I was in vet school, I was contacted by a friend of the family who said she had a sister who worked for the university and had a house with horses nearby. This sister, Mrs. Wendy, had a farm fifteen minutes outside of town, down several dirt roads and over a single-lane bridge. She was looking for a responsible young person to watch over her many animals and large farm when she and her husband were out of town. I was thrilled to be considered for this; jobs in vet school that were manageable were hard to come by, and an opportunity to ride horses for free was an exponential blessing for me. In the years to come, what I did not realize right away was that Ms. Wendy would become more—young-person crisis counselor, Christian mentor, family away from home, and invaluable friend for life.

I had at this point one year of vet school under my belt, but the high levels of stress were having an effect on me. I was in a bit of a desperate search for positive outlets in which to turn my restless anxiety when the relentless tests would let up for a brief moment. I would spend many a sleepless night forcibly plunging large masses of information into my brain. Often, the next day after the test, I would find myself exhausted, but unable to sleep, wanting large amounts of chocolate and more coffee. My brain was subliminally trying to find something with joy attached to it. I like running a lot, but it was not anywhere near the brain candy I needed as riding a horse was after big tests. Later, I would find that planting flowers was also a positive diversion, and watching them grow was so satisfying. Just FYI to those of you who have never tried gardening. But I digress.

Now, in my second year of vet school, I was overjoyed about this perfect opportunity for me, but little did I realize it would lead to a craziness I have not witnessed since.

Wendy greeted me as my grandma's 1982 Pontiac 6000, now my vehicle, pulled into her farm. Her smile, our family ties, and her obvious love of her animals made conversation and friendship very easy, as it so often does. She gave me a grand tour of her place, a log cabin mansion built by her husband into the side of a hill. She carefully introduced me to every dog—an Irish setter, a Schnauzer, two Basset hounds and an old Doberman, each of which had a special story and special needs. Then she walked me down to the barn.

The barn was built with multiple levels and high rafters. Inside were three horses, all relatively young. The first, Miss Scarlet, greeted me with the kindest of snorts, slow and inquisitive but eager to be pals. I gently greeted her back. She was a beautiful bay, four-year-old half thoroughbred and half Arabian. She had modest height and the classic Arab dish face. The second horse, a two-year-old male Arabian named Alizar, seemed more shy and spirited. Wendy explained that he was very minimally saddle broke, probably not the best to start out with. The third horse was a chestnut quarter horse who was sassy and temperamental, and seemed to be the leader of this pack. Her name was Rose, and her greeting was short, but cordial. I knew I would have some work to do to win her over, but it was a welcome challenge.

For now, I was just so excited for my opportunity, a wonderful gift. And that's the moment when I saw him, standing in the aisle, an unlikely animal. He kept strolling around the aisle of the barn.

"What's that?" I asked, pointing to an odd bird that vaguely resembled a chicken or maybe a small turkey.

"Oh, that's Chucks, or at least that's what I call him. Isn't he neat?"

I stared; he was gray and uniformly covered in white dots. I paused for a moment, because the next question may not be very becoming of a vet student, a supposedly pseudo expert on all things animal, and here I was, with a potential employer, but since I had no idea...

"Yes, ma'am, his feathers are beautiful, but what is he?" I asked.

"He's a guinea fowl. He wandered up a few days ago. I am not sure where he came from, but he seems to like the barn area."

"Do I take care of him too?"

"Well, he's been eating the horse feed, but I finally went and got him some proper bird food. Just throw him some feed when you are out here feeding, and he'll be happy, if you are taking care of everything."

"Okay, sure."

I looked at Chucks; he eyed me back.

I spoke briefly with Mrs. Wendy about when her first out-of-town trips would be, and then she asked me when I would be out to ride. I said I think next week after some exams would be good; I felt comfortable with everything.

"Who would you like to ride first?" she asked me.

"I think it would be easiest just to begin with Miss Scarlett? Her temperament is so kind and wonderful and she is just a bit older than Alizar. What do you think?"

"I think that sounds perfect," said Mrs. Wendy.

The following week, I got out of exams and excitedly put on my riding breeches and boots, which had not been worn much at all in recent years. It was a beautiful sunny day. I crossed the one-lane bridge over the beautiful creek below, and I felt the excitement building. It was a great day; I have a break from testing, and I was going to do something exciting, positive, and healthy.

I met Miss Scarlett at the barn. She greeted me with the same kind curiosity as before. I gently coaxed her on to the cross ties and began to go through my entire grooming ritual, which I have richly enjoyed since young-girl years. It was all so relaxing. Miss Scarlett seemed to enjoy the brushing and tending to; she obeyed me when I asked for her hooves to tend to them and obediently lifted when I asked. The other two horses watched from across the paddock but did not seem as interested in my activities. Chucks, on the other hand, remained close by, watching carefully.

I spoke to Miss Scarlett, and she seemed to understand my conversation. Her ears flickered back and forth. I placed the saddle on her carefully; she had not been ridden in months, but she seemed to be content with the process. I placed the reins over her head, and she gently accepted the bit to her bridle. "Good girl," I cooed and patted her. *She is wonderful,* I thought.

The ring for riding was a quarter of a mile away from the stable area, so I decided to walk her down and mount up in the pasture. I slowly left the stable area with Miss Scarlet obediently walking alongside, and I was careful to latch the gate behind me. As I walked through some beautiful foliage, I glanced about, thankful for the day and the small pleasures God had provided me—an answer to a prayer.

I glanced back; the bird had followed us. I stared at it. *Odd.* I stopped at the gate, and Chucks stopped next to Miss Scarlet, by her feet. I thought for sure the bird would just wander back to the stable after a while. I let Miss Scarlett in the pasture and shut the gate so Chucks was on the other side. I did not want him to spook Miss Scarlett. I was, after all, riding by myself on a horse I had never ridden and which had not been ridden for months. Not exactly ideal. As I began to mount up on her, I swung my leg over carefully and noticed Chucks had jumped up on the fence and was cackling some.

I wish that thing would go away...grrr...oh well.

I walked Scarlett carefully around the pasture; she seemed delighted by it all. I started just in a small circle by the gate and then became a bit adventurous as she was so delightful and responsive to ride. I decided to trot her some, and she gleefully bounded forward in a modest yet energetic trot. I was watching all I was doing and had not noticed the cackling had become worse. It didn't seem to bother Scarlett at all.

I decided to trot around the pasture and took off away from the fence line. Out of the corner of my eye, I saw the bird fly off the fence line and come screeching after us. He was screaming and running behind Scarlett with his wings outstretched and his legs furiously trying to keep up. The screeching became worse and worse. There was an agony in this ridiculous creature that I did not understand. I stopped Scarlett and stared at Chucks. Clearly, he was confused by this riding business and me, but why would a bird care?

I hushed at Chucks and walked Scarlett quietly for a moment to try to calm this lunatic bird, who was still wings up, carrying on in circles, screeching like the sky was falling.

I decided to try to ride a bit longer. Maybe the bird would calm down and let me be since, actually, there was really nothing to be upset over. I kept trotting Scarlett in small circles; she still seemed delighted in the commands and unaffected by Chucks. Chucks quieted some but relentlessly kept up trotting behind us. He started to look a bit weary, and I was glad for it. Back to trying to enjoy my riding day, without a squawking, cackling, crazed avian acting like I was ripping away his best and closest friend. *Ridiculous.*

Eventually, after twenty to twenty-five minutes, I felt I should not overdo Miss Scarlett on this, our first outing. She had been so good, despite lunatic Chucks going nuts over it. I patted her neck, grateful, and dismounted.

I carefully walked her back to the barn, petting her neck. Occasionally, I would glance behind us for the crazy bird who insisted on remaining clingy to me and Miss Scarlett. I glanced at him. *Some horses might've tried to take a swift hoof to you, fella, with all of that nonsense and carrying-on.*

I got back to the stable. I carefully removed the tack from Miss Scarlet and brushed her some. Mrs. Wendy greeted me; she had come home from her teaching job at the university. She glanced at Scarlett and me.

"I just came down to feed. How was it?" she beamed.

I remained positive and thankful, but added I had some trouble with the bird.

"Oh no! I should've warned you about that!"

"What is he, like…attached to the horse?" I squinched my nose and furrowed my brow, obviously confused by the squawking bird dilemma.

"Oh well, actually…They're in love."

"What?! A horse and a guinea fowl?" I tried to absorb this casual explanation.

"Yes, it's very funny."

"I wondered why the bird was going crazy."

"Well, yeah, you were stealing his girl."

"Oh, but no way, I mean does Scarlett ever get irritated by it?"

"Oh no, she loves him back."

"What?!"

"Come here and watch." Mrs. Wendy waved at me, and we went and hid behind a stable door. If I had not seen what followed, I would not be writing about it today.

Miss Scarlett was in her stall, quietly eating her hay that was mounted to the right of the door. Chucks awkwardly flew up to the top of her stall door, spread his wings wide and began a more soothing cooing toward Miss Scarlett, obviously courting her in his own way.

Miss Scarlett took a brief pause from her dinner to address her suitor. She gently took her muzzle and carefully nuzzled his chest for several moments, which overwhelmed and exhilarated Chucks into more romance noises and wings-spread dances. I stared in disbelief and could only offer a chuckle. Then Mrs. Wendy and I quietly exited, leaving them to their romance, the most unlikely I have ever encountered.

Meanwhile, back at the shelter...

Kitty Mutt waited for the woman on the other end of the line to speak; she had been a client for a few years, been to the clinic a few times with her cat—Ms. Maddie Curl. She was middle aged, an unkempt type, and usually quiet. Finally, the woman's voice came to life on the other end of the phone line. She took a gasp of air as she began her frantic tale: "I rented a house that had recently become infested with aliens." She paused, then she slowly spoke in a whisper, "I see the aliens mostly at night, but sometimes, they run through my house during the day."

"Um, okay," Kitty Mutt acknowledged with a smile. "How do you know they are aliens?"

"Oh well, the aliens are pooping in the cat's litter box. I know that the feces belong to the aliens and not to the cat because their poop is different, like glue. They poop a sticky, slimy goo that is very hard to scrub out of the litter box."

Kitty contemplated on how best to angle her next set of questions.

The Lab Who Knew

When I was reaching the end of the vet school career, I went on a preceptorship for three months to a clinic that treated horses and small animals. It's like an internship for students about to graduate. It was just right for me and my interests. It was located in the country, which was a good place to start. I came across a Labrador that was a bit of a marvel, but not for any health-related reason at all.

It has been many years, and I am writing this with the perspective of a seasoned veterinarian. It might take a veterinarian to appreciate it. Often, it can be a bit depressing, but some animals don't really like the vet's clinic where they get all the pokes. Vets do not make many animal friends with fecal loops and thermometers. I would imagine it would be hard for most animals, especially if they were already apprehensive to begin with, to understand that their vet is motivated by a love for animals. It's what got us to school. Some pets are just easy; the cuddling and petting gestures that I offer way outweigh the few little sticks that follow. They still like me.

Occasionally, I meet that one patient that sticks the sore paw out for you, that looks at you with some understanding that you are trying to help them. I love this. They have a knowing look; they offer a submissive stance, while you are checking a catheter or checking their anemia level for the eighth time with a poke. I believe I saw the look often in horse colic as they would sigh relief after a Banamine injection for pain. I spoke of it often after eye removal surgery, enucleation, where you remove an eye due to profound enlargement and disease. Sounds horrible, but there is no other option in some cases. One hundred percent of the cats I performed this surgery on were purring, eating, and rubbing on their cages and me the next day. It's not always that you get that thank-you look, but it's sure nice when you do.

I had a pet one day that got me; he got who I was. I was there to help him.

He was an unlikely candidate.

I was at my new job as an intern-like person of sorts; a preceptor is what the position is called. It was in a mixed-animal practice in a rural mountain community. They had four vets who rotated, being on call, and had all the routine equipment. They were all good mentors for me, the budding veterinarian, about to graduate. They had a lineup of drop-off cases. They gave me the drop-offs to keep me busy and help me get my feet wet. This also kept me out of the spotlight with the clients until I had been broken in some. I had made it through a few cases when I saw one marked "check eye"—the eye of Buddy Martin, a two-year-old chocolate Lab.

I waited for the kennel help to get him. All the dogs set off barking before I could see him. Sounded like a giant ruckus. Buddy came bouncing out of the kennel area and into the treatment area, giddy with delight. He ignored the person hanging on to his lead and ran to every person who was working to greet them and inappropriately sniff them. He must've been one hundred pounds of brawn and glory. He surged right and then surged left. He was a Lab and a mighty joyous one at that. He had minimal respect for a leash and a tail that was so happy it was slapping everybody and everything. The kennel helper brought him to me as I tried to begin. I had to say hello to Buddy for five minutes or more till he was somewhat satisfied that we were acquainted.

I sighed a little. Check eye. It's not easy on a bounding Lab or energetic or scared or nervous pet of any sort.

I thought of my protocol I had been taught on ophthalmology: four tests, usually. The tests are stain eye to check for corneal ulcers, eye pressures for glaucoma, foreign bodies under the third eyelid and conjunctiva, check for adequate tear production. The history said he had been running in the farm fields most days.

I looked at this eye. His right eye had a stream of excessive tears that had dried on the right side of his muzzle. They were clear tears.

43

He licked my face, still super excited. I got out the ophthalmoscope to look; nothing seemed abnormal within the globe of the eye. I moved right and then left as Buddy still wanted to watch everybody else. Buddy squinted occasionally with his right eye, but it did not appear tremendously painful. I decided he probably didn't need a tear test since they were streaming quite nicely out of this eye. He was a bit young for glaucoma, and the instrument we used to check eye pressure was adequate, but it looked like a torture device out of the Dark Ages, with a metal circle and a pin/needle, and you must get just right over the eye. Buddy was not a great candidate unless maybe he had full anesthesia, a bit extreme.

I decided we would look for foreign bodies in the conjunctiva and stain the eye for possible corneal ulcers. Hopefully, he would settle some.

I got all my tests together; Buddy was excited and watched me eagerly. As I came close to put a drop of proparacaine, a local anesthetic, in his eye, I realized this was the first time I am touching the right eye with my fingertips.

Buddy became extremely still. He restrained all his explosive energies and was barely breathing. I looked at him. He stared at me with his right eye toward me.

"Wow, you okay, Buddy?" He was very quiet. A small tail wag was all that remained. I looked at the holder, and she just stared, perplexed, but encouraged me, waving her hand: *Just take advantage!*

Using a moistened sterile Q-tip, I searched around the conjunctiva, the pink inside the eyelids. Top, bottom—nothing. Buddy was being so good.

As I proceeded, Buddy did not move a muscle in his face, body, or head. I was right next to him, in his eyeball. He kept his tail to the most restricted tail wag. He had become a statue for me. It was like he was perched with his eye directly on me.

I was taught by my professors to always lift the third eyelid and check under, just in case there was an object caught.

So here's my crazy. I let go of the eye for a moment to make certain this very still dog was okay. As I pulled back an inch, Buddy leaned toward me, right eye forward. He wanted me to keep on. He did not blink; he was keeping his eyelids open, so I could look?

CRAZY, *but totally great…*

I gently brought my Q-tip under the conjunctiva and lifted the third eyelid to peek behind it. Buddy held his breath.

There it was, the culprit—a large hay seed stuck in the corner of his eye. Slowly and carefully, I was able to coax/scoop it out of its hiding place. It was like a small glorious treasure, especially to a young vet. I marveled at it as soon as I got it out. Buddy immediately shook his head, blinked his eye, and completely resorted to his previous excitement jollies with tail slapping and tongue lagging. The kennel holder was unable to hang on.

He seemed to celebrate with me in utter elation. He stuck his wet nose in my face and licked it; I laughed. I would not be able to express how a Lab tried to help me get a seed out of his eye for many years. It was when I realized that a pet aiding you with an understanding to be still, especially one like that, was not the norm.

I had to quiet him down to check his eyes for corneal ulcers, but he was so relieved, he did not see the point in being still anymore. His problem was fixed; he was ready to go. He was negative for the ulcer stain. I sent him home with some ointment, just in case the tissues had become irritated from the seed. I never saw him again, but I didn't forget.

He knew.

In a Snowstorm

Now, I had been single for several years, but I had a boyfriend in college and a fun time on the dating scene since then. I went out one night my third year of vet school and ended up in super lousy situation with a vet student who was much too eager, and I had to leave, much to his dismay.

I, being very frustrated, decided to pray for my future husband, in detail. It was Novemberish, and I was a bit down about it all.

I was at my parents' house for Thanksgiving. I had been out of the local crowds for over six years since I had gone to an out-of-state school. I watched my sister, who was two years younger, chatting with all her friends. Being bored with TV and not wanting to try to pick up the phone and awkwardly reunite with high school folks, I asked her, "Hey, Raegan, can I come along?"

Raegan, my sister, was surprised, excitedly said yes, and called five more people. All her friends had gone to the same in-state university and ran together ever since high school. I had chosen a different path, but I loved my school. However, all these guys and gals were super welcoming, like family; they knew I wasn't in town very often due to vet school.

We all made plans to go out that night. The first person at my house was a fellow named Marshall. He had a big smile and was full of fun. He knew all the college crowd we were about to hang out with, but for some reason, our paths had never crossed. He had been at my house many, many times. He knew my brother and my parents. He had never been more than friends with my sister and her friends. They (my family and my sister's friends) had witnessed a massive transformation in Marshall, which I had missed out on completely, being that I went to a different college in a different state and now was in a completely consuming vet program.

46

He sat at the bar in my parent's kitchen, making fun of my sister and me. His sarcasm seemed brutally endless. We could not stop laughing; it was beginning to hurt my sides. I said to her, "Who is your friend? He's so fun."

She saw my interest and gave me a shocked expression that said, "Really? You think so?"

Uncertain but hopeful, I said, "Yeah, kinda…"

We went to a party with friends, and he just kept talking to me about everything. It was so easy. All my sister's friends kept staring and shaking their heads, "Marshall and Raegan's sister, June, the vet student? That's so weird, but whatever."

I learned a lot about this interesting guy, Marshall. He had paid and studied his way through two years of community college to achieve his dream of attending a major university. Prior to community college, you could say he had a couple of major hardships and a poor track record in high school that had gotten him off course. He was determined to come back. He had lost a bunch of weight by working out (over a hundred pounds) and managed to quit smoking just before that. He was a growing Christian, like me. Marshall had just finished his first semester at a major university, his long-awaited goal, and he had a 4.0 GPA. I love a comeback story. He was feelin' good, I noticed, plus he was fun, and the conversation just never ended.

Finally, I went home. What a great night. I could not stop the fun vibe I had inside me. I told Marshall I would look forward to the next time we got to go out together. It was just what I needed after a lousy social event just a few weeks earlier. That was Thanksgiving.

I got home for Christmas after all my vet school finals and was hopeful that maybe Mr. Marshall would call me again or stop by. *Hmmm hope so…*

My sister told me he was really excited to see me, but there was a giant snowstorm blocking him from getting home from the university. I hadn't given him my number or anything. We got a call from a guy friend that Marshall was on the highway, battling the storm in his Toyota truck to get home. Raegan said, "Why? He should've stayed where he was!"

"Well," he said, "I am pretty sure he wants to say hi to your sister."

Oh, goodness.

He showed up an hour later. It was a bit awkward. His mom only lived three miles away, but he had come to our house first. I was impressed (and super flattered). Later, when I would meet his mom, this same woman would ask me, "Why Marshall? You seem like such a nice girl." (He does have a bit of a problem with being too sarcastic.)

Because he made me laugh.

We dated long distance after that. He would come and hang with my vet school buddies. Most of my close friends had come to recognize him as a fun, interesting guy. We had a party at my place one night, and he noticed a group of my fourth-year classmates he had not met before. They were country boys, and they were big on cattle. They all had manure stains at the top of their shoulders, all of them, and they were proud. Hard at it all day, they said. They had been practicing the fine bovine art of rectal palpation, important for reproduction reasons.

To do this, bovine rectal palpation, you put on a long glove up to the shoulder, go into the cow rectally, and calculate where the uterus is in its cycle or whether the cow is pregnant. It's an import-ant bovine vet thing, especially for those wishing to become bovine vets. We even have vet school competitions for it (palpation teams). They are always trying to practice to win at nationals—no joke. They showed their stains to Marshall like they had just fixed Mario Andretti's car and the grease was still on 'em. It made them very pow-erful among vet students (just kidding). Marshall stared and said, "Oh, sure man!" Marshall never forgot. Rich with sarcasm, he asked me to explain why they were so proud of their stains many, many times. Poor nonveterinary folk, it's hard to understand us sometimes.

Mostly, Marshall would just come visit me and go fishing at the nearby lakes. My dog, Camper, really liked him. After a while, he would begin to understand that when I said I would be done in twenty minutes with my vet cases, that really meant like two hours.

A year later, Marshall had gone to great lengths to hang a giant sign on a building. He worked hard all day with his father to get an old boat running so he could take me to see the sign. We made it out on the Mississippi River in downtown Memphis. Just to go for a "boat ride." We made it to where he'd hung the sign. It had partially fallen when he showed it to me; it just said "JUNE," and the rest was lost in a twisted curl. "What does it say?" I asked him…completely oblivious. I could not imagine it to be a major event. I looked at him; he was so flustered. Confused, I shrugged my shoulders. Then Marshall, my fantastic diamond in the rough, got on one knee and asked me to marry him.

Chiropractor Visit

T he year was 2000, and I had graduated vet school. The first town I started practicing veterinary medicine in was beautiful, with a lot of animals in need, I'll call this place Nicefolksville, USA. I came to this job in the most unusual of ways. Most jobs in veterinary medicine are found through various channels: vet magazines with help wanted ads, vet websites with job ads, and I have spoken to headhunters before. There were many vets who had called the vet school looking for good recommendations from professors. The large veterinary companies came by to interview graduating students. These are the ways most veterinary positions are filled.

My first job came about because my dad, an airplane pilot, was talking about me at his chiropractor's office. He had stopped by for an adjustment and was chatting with the receptionist who, after years of seeing my dad come in and out, asked about the routine things, the normal chatter. He mentioned I was graduating from vet school. She seemed so intrigued. "Ya know," she said, "my brother-in-law is a vet. He really needs some help. She should call him, he works with horses and small animals. He's just two hours away. Here's his number. He's a nice guy, she should call him."

And that was it—not your average job search. I had gone to several interviews set up by my professors and gotten two or three job offers that seemed exciting but not quite right. In the end, I decided that the chiropractor's brother-in-law was the perfect job for me with an experienced veterinarian, Dr. Grey Quarter.

Ten Amish Brothers and a Dead Battery

All stared—ten Amish brothers—at me. They, standing in a lineup toward me, watching...me? Hand inside mare's birthing equipment.

Well, this is awesome.

"So do you all tend to the horses?" I tried painfully to disrupt the staring and the silence. They simultaneously nodded.

Nicefolksville is a small American town where I began my career. Its uniqueness lay in the fact that it was home to many Amish residents. The Amish were often seen in carriages on the country roads. They made their way into town regularly, most often to visit the chiropractor—a luxury they enjoyed. It was not uncommon to see an occasional carriage go through Main Street, or to drive up behind one going down a country road. The Amish residents also really loved Walmart. The retail giant had beautifully embraced this relationship by including horse-drawn-wagon parking spaces. The horse carriage parking was clearly and conveniently marked, located near the front doors of Walmart, with clean water troughs off to the side. To this vet's approval, it was complete with a nice place to tie the horses and buggies.

Occasionally, the clinic received calls from Amish country. These calls were usually about a particularly ill horse and/or a choppy situation filled with odd anecdotes. Some treatments included rectally placed onions (ouch), or beer to increase urination.

An Amish man called about a retained placenta in a mare who had aborted her foal over twenty-four hours ago. If the afterbirth or retained placenta is not expelled by a horse within four hours, the situation becomes an emergency. If left untreated, often what will follow is a deadly foot condition called founder. This poor mare's placenta had been hanging attached since yesterday.

I drove out at dusk to the Amish community and found the farm. I had not responded to a vet call in their neck of the woods in the two months I had been working in Nicefolksville. The farm had a long, wooded dirt and gravel drive with well-worn carriage tracks up to a large house. The house, a simple white two-story home, sat on a hill overlooking the farm. The house was big with a large country front porch and steps to the front door. There was a barn off to the right that seemed a bit worn, and in the middle of a field, and half mile in the distance, was a mill that also looked much like a wooden barn shed.

This is where I met the ten brothers, all with no beards, which, in the Amish world, signifies not yet married. As I pulled in, I saw them jumping down off the porch, coming up from the barn and around from the back of the house. All at once, they stood together, ten young Amish males, ranging from ten to twenty years of age, quietly staring—at me.

Deep breath, start with simple:

"Hello, I'm, Dr. French. Is there a Mr. Clyde Dale here? We received a call for a mare who could not pass her afterbirth."

They all stared and smiled from ear to ear.

"I'm a veterinarian from Dr. Quarter's office."

Hmm…do they speak English? Did my boss say something about them speaking Danish, or maybe German? I can't remember.

Finally, the awkward silence ceased. The oldest brother, spoke.

"Clyde Dale went to a meeting tonight. He is our father. We'll be helping you tonight."

He stared at me. He offered a big smile. "I'm Matthew. I am the **oldest** brother."

I nodded and smiled back.

"So, are you all brothers?"

They all nodded.

I asked for reasons of pure unexpected curiosity, possibly inappropriately and due to being a premature suburban-raised girl. "So, the same mom had all ten of you boys?" I smiled.

They seemed to have been asked that before, as they were moderately humored and answered again with a nod.

Wow, that woman!

"Okay, so you have a mare with a retained placenta?"

"Yes," said Matthew.

"Well, would you like me to look at her?"

"Oh yes, of course. We'll show you to the barn," he responded.

"Can I pull my truck up there?" I asked, surveying the distance to the barn and the gate in the way.

"Oh yes!"

Evidently, all the brothers understood that, because they all ran for the gate to open it.

Well, chivalry is definitely being taught here in Amish country. I wonder if they have ever seen a female vet before—maybe not.

The mare was a sweet girl. A large bay carriage horse, Standard bred. She quietly let me examine her. She did not appear to have the dreaded laminitis disease setting in yet. She had aborted her foal prematurely at four to five months of pregnancy yesterday. Normal pregnancy for a mare is eleven months.

I started to treat this mare. In my young career, I had faced this emergency before, I gave her some oxytocin to help induce uterine contractions. I also gave her some Banamine to help with discomfort and to absorb endotoxins, or toxins that lead to laminitis. I told the brothers what I was doing because they were watching me curiously and quietly.

Matthew said proudly, "We have oxytocin injectable. We gave her some yesterday, but nothing happened." He went over to the shelf and grabbed a dust-covered injectable medication.

"Oh well, it might be expired, because it should be kept in a cool place, like a refrigerator. Is it always here in the barn year around? It should be kept cold." I made polite observations about their medicine.

"Yes, you think it was no good?" Matthew asked concerned.

"Do you keep it here in the barn in the summer?"

Matthew nodded. The brothers quietly stared from me to him and back to me.

"Yes, probably not any good anymore." He showed me the bottle, which was a year expired or more and should have never been out of a refrigerator. Heat ruins the drug.

I put my long glove on and up my arm went into the mare's backside birthing equipment. I stood with my arm trying to get her afterbirth free while ten young men stared intently at me. For some reason that could only be related to the obvious male-female scenario, I was trying desperately to avoid the word *vaginal*, but it was difficult to avoid discussing this anatomical feature of the horse at that moment.

After multiple minutes of silence, I asked the boys if they like horses, because I could think of nothing else for conversation. Matthew began rambling on about how much he knew about horses. He talked about their feeding schedules and how often he checked their water. He told me about how he learned about their hoof care and their breeding schedules. He went on to tell me he also knew about tooth care from a friend teaching him how to file horse teeth. In veterinary medicine, we call this "floating," but I just quietly nodded.

Great, Matthew, great. Right now I am glad that there is no awkward silence. So I will continue to act impressed by your horse knowledge, so you will hopefully just keep talking.

He was surprisingly full of horsey conversation. Yet I remained somewhat uneasy since after all, I was literally up to my elbow in the horse's birthing, i.e. vaginal, equipment, by myself with ten males observing me and the horse. What sensible person does this? A question I will often ask myself in future experiences as well.

Perhaps it was the long time she had the afterbirth in her, but getting the afterbirth to detach from the mare's uterus with my gentle tension methods proved to be very difficult. I was using every technique available. You have to go slow, with the mare's contractions, and gently peel the afterbirth apart from the uterine lining. If you leave some afterbirth pieces in the mare, you may still end up with a founder problem.

So I proceeded slowly with ten pairs of eyes on me. It had become really dark outside. Periodically, to busy myself and to break up intermittent silences, I took my arm out of the mare's vaginal canal, took off my glove and ran over to the vet box on the back of the truck to look at my supplies. The vet truck, which had a small light on, was a momentary escape and recollection, as it was taking too long to get the afterbirth out of the mare. At the truck, I would quietly pick up more scrubbing and uterine flushing materials. I was also trying to create the impression that I had an important objective in mind when really I was dealing with my own anxiety.

Why is this taking so long? So many stares...

Among my supplies, I found an aid: a flashlight! It was very dark both outside and inside the barn. I was in Amish country.

After a lifetime of extended efforts, actually two hours, I succeeded. The mare contracted, and the afterbirth slid out in its entirety. I experienced a leap for joy in my brain. I finished treating the mare with some more flushes to her uterus. I went back to my truck, closed the supply lid, but failed to notice that the small light to my supplies had gone out. I thanked everyone. They enthusiastically thanked me. They said their father would stop by the clinic tomorrow to pay. Great! Wonderful! I was finished. Or so I imagined!

That's when I tried to start my truck. It was dead. The battery to my vet truck had died at the very end of my extended treatment efforts. I now know one of the most inconvenient places to have a dead battery. I tried multiple times to start the truck. Again the ten brothers stared. They whispered amongst themselves. They got excited when they remembered they had a lawn mower battery at their mill. They eagerly went to get it. I was thankful for this piece of hope but a little skeptical; after all, I was driving a rather large farm truck. They got the battery; I had cables. We tried. No success. I think the brothers were more disappointed than me.

So, I asked for the phone. No phone on an Amish farm was the answer. *Oh yes, somehow, I need to gain more Amish insight—note to self.* The farm was fifteen miles away from the clinic, it was 11:00 p.m., and the whole area was strange territory to me.

"What should I do?"

"Well, mmm...walk back?"

Oh dear.

Matthew offered to walk with me to the nearest house that had a phone and electricity. We set out. Completely uncomfortable with my circumstances, eyes wide with forced walking steps, I prayed under my breath. He kept chatting with me. Down the long gravel drive we walked. Thankfully, the moon offered some light.

Then it happened. He asked me if I had a special fellow in my life.

"What?" I asked, both astounded and confused.

"Do ya have a special feller in your life that you're seein'? Ya know, a boyfriend?"

He stared at me with a hopeful smile.

"Well, actually, yes…" I tried to meet the question and his unexpected curiosity into my personal life. "I am going to be married in about a month." I smiled, it was true. I waited for a "best wishes" type of response, but no.

He looked at me, puzzled and disappointed. He pleaded, as we were walking, "Oh no, you needn't rush into all that. You should be more sure about it," he said directly.

I told Matthew I was sure about it. I was very uncomfortable and annoyed.

Then, in a hopeful voice, he added, "Well, you know, you still have time."

For what?

To marry someone else?

I looked over at him, and he flashed a big, charming smile, adding, "Ya know, there are other fellers out there."

(Insert totally awkward moment when I realize that the Amish boy who is walking with me has a romantic interest.)

He switched back to trying to impress me with his horse knowledge. He told me where his father gets his fine horses from and that sometimes he gets to go and help with the horses. I tried stealthily to pick up the walking pace.

We reached the little ranch house with its electricity and telephone service. We explained our situation to the nice couple, who let me use the phone. When I told Dr. Quarter where I was and what had happened, the husband of this couple mentioned that he had a similar-model truck and offered to give me a jump. I recall my boss approving before he added, "Yes, I noticed the battery acting up this week. I guess I should have said something."

Bravely, I, the modern neighbor man, and my very friendly Amish fella loaded up in a large Ford pickup. When we broke out the cables and jumped the vet truck, it roared back to life. I gulped a huge breath of relief.

I waved good-bye, rejoicing inside while trying to keep my poise. I thanked the neighbor man, the Amish boys, the good Lord, and off I went, out of Amish land, away from the ten polite, bare-chinned brothers, one of which—I think—thought well of me.

My First Cat Lady Encounter

It was my second week on the job, and I came in the hospital to find my boss in an exam room giving fluid therapy to a thin cat, with an owner sitting nearby. The fluids were being given subcutaneously, which means just under the skin, to help rehydrate. This feline had a serious condition called lymphoma, an aggressive form of cancer. The client was pleased to meet me, but Dr. Quarter seemed worried for me. The woman, Mrs. Bengal, had long silver hair that was nicely spun up into a bun on top of her head, make-up on and was well dressed. She was probably 75 -80 years old, although I never did ask her, of course. She was a thin lady. She had a big smile and offered a welcoming greeting. Hi, I am Dr. June French.

She talked about how she had been to the university oncology vet school department to save this cat. He was not doing well, but he was a very special cat. I was pleased to meet an owner who cared so much. After I left the room, Dr. Quarter came out and looked at me and said, "You better just let me deal with her, she's complicated. If you get her on call, I'm sorry."

"Why?" I said. "She seems nice, takes good care of her kitty there, despite a poor prognosis. Went all the way to the university for chemotherapy."

"Yeah, well," he said skeptically, rolling his eyes, trying to con-figure a description for this owner.

Then he looked at me and slowly whispered to me just of hint of all that was to come that year. "I'm just not sure how many cats she actually has."

Well, with a smile, I asked, "Have you tried asking?"

"Yeah, I don't get an answer." Then he continued in a whisper, "I'm not sure *she knows*."

Oh my.

It was a foreshadowing of at least one hundred cases to come that year.

Over time, I would realize how funny, trying, and sometimes perplexing this was. It would start as a small trickle of simple cases.

The first few cases she would ask me about, and bring them to me. She seemed uncertain, but I was eager to prove that I was a knowledgeable professional and gain the confidence of this eclectic client. Plus, I actually love feline medicine. Usually, she said the cat was new. It was negative for most of the common diseases. Typically, they just had upper respiratory infections. I would put them on antibiotics. She would tell me they were doing fine, but she never brought them in for rechecks. She slowly seemed more confident in my abilities, and I was always excited when the clients, especially this one, began to trust me. Be careful what you wish for. This happy skipping slowly changed into a slow plod with weighted feet in the trenches of the feline world.

Like a slow downhill slope, it got more involved. Late in the fall, Mrs. Bengal started bringing me cats with injuries like abscesses and puncture wounds. These things are still routine to treat and fairly common in multiple-cat houses. I tested these cats every time I got ahold of them for feline leukemia and feline AIDS (FIV), but they were always negative. I was sure one of these days she was going to get a cat that was positive. I felt I was gaining in strides as a veterinarian. I was proving I was worthy of her pet's care. It was so important to me that I be accepted. I kept treating ear mites and dental problems. Then she started to catch me more on the weekends. I rarely remember seeing the same cat twice, but I had Mrs. Bengal's glowing approval of my professional abilities. I started to casually ask if we have all her cats on record, for vaccine reasons. I never got a real answer. Dr. Quarter's original concern would float back and forth in my mind...*How many are there?*

I pressed on with administering care for Mrs. Bengal's brood, but it became more challenging, a challenge that was not very welcome to a rookie.

From February to June, Mrs. Bengal presented me with an onslaught of cancer cases: mammary cancer in two cases, so I took the cats to surgery and spayed them. I explained to her that this was related to a lack of being spayed. Then she had two cats that presented in respiratory distress one week apart. I had a few cases of a fungal disease in dogs called blastomycosis. I once or twice wondered if these two cats of Mrs. Bengal's might have it too. We ended up doing humane euthanasia for both and sent them out to the state lab. They both had advanced cancer spread all over their lungs, confirmed at the state lab. I felt so bad to repeatedly dish out pathology reports that were so horrible. It got to where I could never give her any good news at all and she would just say, "It's okay, I'm used to it."

Each cat was special and had a special place in her life. She would specify them all as an individual. Eventually, it became a challenge to keep up. I couldn't remember all their names. She never was limited on funds for each case, which was uncommon for this rural town. I encouraged her to look into her house for possible environmental hazards, seriously, because there were so many cats that had metastatic cancer. She would just smile and nod like I was crazy. She would tell me, "But me and my husband are fine!"

I guess at eighty years old, that's a reasonable thing to say.

There were reports that she would go around town and pick up one or two cans of cat food from each local store. She would do this every day as part of her routine. She would stand and stew at the counters in front of store clerks every day over whether to go with a beef based or a seafood. Clearly she was entertaining picky feline eaters, but was it just one or one hundred? I am not sure about her other food sources because the cats never looked underfed; maybe she did it all day long. No one really knows.

Toward the end of the year, Dr. Quarter found me frustrated again in the middle of looking at another Mrs. Bengal's sick cat. I was shaking my head. It had all spiraled from a nice friendship and rewarding treatments to a giant monster full of complicated medicine. I did not enjoy communicating bad news. He looked at me and said, "Did you figure it out yet?"

Thinking he was talking about the case, I said no and vented about all that I thought could be wrong and the diagnostics that I had run. I was pulling my hair out.

"No," he said. "Did you figure out how many cats she has?"
I thought about this.
"Well no, but I believe I have an answer…"
His eyebrows perked up.
"Really?" he said, "How many?"
"Too many, too, too many."
He laughed.
My patient mentor of a boss had had this experience with this client every year for over twenty-five years. That poor guy.

Grandma Can't Sew

In every private vet practice, there is the Saturday. It is usually a
shortened day—nine to noon or nine to three, that type of thing.
However, it remains a day for craziness because it is convenient for
folks who work during the week. So Saturdays in vet medicine are a
little crazy, even more so if you are a new graduate and you're on for
the day, by yourself. Potentially and often massively overwhelming.

We had at our practice multiple college-age students who would
work weekends and summers, trying to figure out if veterinary medicine was a field for them. They were productive, dependable, and
fun. I had a fellow named Joey, a longtime local, my first year in practice who had worked at the clinic for some time. He knew how to
work every machine and find anything I needed, even remote farms.
A very handy person. He was always laughing about something and
often full of jokes and, occasionally, a good prank. We had a second
college student; we'll call her Nancy. She chatted a lot, knew everyone in town, was good with animals, and was fairly knowledgeable
in basic medicine. We had fun, despite the craziness and difficult
situations that were often handed to us.

Now, on one fine Saturday, I was at the clinic. The rooms were
packed. The appointments were every fifteen minutes. I got in that
morning, took a deep breath, and as I often do, I would say a small
prayer before the craziness all began.

Also, on this particular day, I was sure Joey had targeted me for
a prank.

Nancy came in midmorning. She was working, but she had
brought along her own pet who was sick. It was a new Chihuahua
puppy. He had been doing great when suddenly, two days ago, he
had just stopped eating completely. Nancy came in to the clinic, and
ran all the routine tests while I was in the exam rooms. She had

already checked this puppy for worms, a virus called parvo, and a "direct" fecal for protozoal parasites before I ever saw it. She told me all this as I came out of an exam room; I still had people waiting. I asked her some basic questions about her puppy while I was looking in microscopes; nothing seemed off. The other doctor had said it was healthy just a few days before.

She said, "I know you are busy in appointments. Is there anything else I can do before you get free to do an exam? I don't want to bug you. I know it's crazy right now."

"Well, I don't think so. If you want, you could have Joey take an X-ray. That might help." Joey heard all this and nodded his head. He was proficient at X-rays. He went back to the treatment area away from the exam rooms. As soon as he was able, he got the little patient and took a quick radiograph of its belly.

I continued my appointments. All was going fairly well; it was mildly chaotic but a fairly controlled morning. (Never say these things in veterinary medicine.)

I came out of a room, and Joey would not let Nancy see the X-ray. He was laughing and smiling and saying, "Not until the doctor sees it first!" She was grabbing, and he was ducking, turning, and wrapping himself around an X-ray film. They were absolutely squabbling like a brother and sister.

Oh my, this can't be good. Joey was acting suspicious; why was he so giddy? He walked over slowly to me. He showed me the X-ray. I immediately saw something impossible on it, and I handed it back to him. "You're playing a joke on me."

He laughed harder, slightly shocked, choked on some saliva, and tried to hand it back to me. I shook my head and fussed. "This is not funny." He said through his laughter, "It's real!"

"No," I said, "it's not, and I am busy, I don't have time for this, Joe. You stuck that thing under the puppy before you shot the X-ray just to watch me freak out when I saw it! I heard you planning this joke a few weeks ago."

I walked off confident and successful not to have been made a fool of. My superkeen senses kept me from falling prey to a prankster, and in the middle of a busy day! Rudeness! I am smart, a professional, and I know what he showed me was not possible.

Right?

He tried terribly to control himself. His face was beet red, and he was shaking his head. Then finally, he tried again. He said more calmly and serious, "Doc, it's real. I promise."

I took a deep breath and looked again. A three-inch-long metal needle in the abdomen of a three-pound Chihuahua puppy—*Oh my gosh*. How on earth did it get there? What dog enjoyed chewing on this? How did this little puppy SWALLOW that? What on earth. The abdomen was probably only about four or five inches across total from the diaphragm to the pelvis. The needle was horizontal across the abdomen on the lateral X-ray. It appeared to be extending from the area of the stomach back to the far-right abdomen (caudal abdomen). Ugh—*sigh*.

(Insert overwhelmed here.)

We carefully took the X-ray back and showed it to Nancy. I said before I showed her, "It's gonna be okay." (Even though I really didn't know for sure.) She had the eye-popping reaction. Joe was probably correct to not to have let her see initially.

She said, "Well, what now?"

I said the only thing I could think of to do. "Well, let's go to surgery."

We finished the appointments while some of the staff got the surgery room ready. I looked at this little guy who didn't look too bad for his situation. We began our procedure. His anesthesia was going well, and I carefully started his exploratory surgery. I discovered how this "foreign body" (as vets call this problem) had come to pass. This puppy had started chewing on the string that was attached to the needle and swallowed the string first and then the needle went down after that. As I was doing the surgery, I realized we had gone to surgery right before the needle had punctured the side of an intestine. A perforation in the intestine could have led to a condition called peritonitis, an infection of the inner lining of the abdomen, which is often fatal. Thankfully, the needle had not yet made it through all the layers, but it was pressed up hard against the wall of the duodenum (small intestine). The needle was too straight and way too large to make a turn in a part of the duodenum called the duodenal flexure (or a sharp turn in the digestive roadway, especially for a three-inch needle). I incised the intestine, removed the needle, and gently coaxed the string out. I sewed the intestine back together and checked for any possible leaks, but he had none. After all the sutures were placed, we woke him up. Ultimately, the surgery outcome was successful.

I still got pranked by Joe routinely, although he never attempted any pranks with X-rays. Nancy had a story that everyone in town knew before the end of two weeks. The good news is the puppy went on to be a normal dog, and Nancy's grandmother was so excited we found her needle and thread. She said she had been missing that.

That Cozy Place

Introducing Dr. Cassie Corgi, my dear friend since my second week of vet school.

Dr. Cassie was working in a rural location in her first month after vet school. Dr. Cassie Corgi is a bright and cheery sort with roots in country living. She has a big smile that goes well with her brown eyes and brunette hair. She has a country accent that could make anyone feel welcome.

She was making her way through room appointments with success and having a fairly steady day. The nurse had been in her next room and, in a rush, told her that it was a new puppy with a skin condition.

"Okay," she said. "I got it!"

She pushed open the door. There sat a rather large woman who was robust in every way. She saw no puppy but extended her hand to introduce herself.

As she did, she saw two little eyes that caught her attention and shocked her to the core.

It was a little Chihuahua nestled deep in a V-neck T-shirt between two giant bosoms. Only his little eyes and nose peeked out.

"Nice to meet you," said the four-hundred-plus-pound owner. She smiled proudly. "This is my new little friend, Rhett. He's very special." She rocked her bosoms back and forth, showcasing their live ornament. *Hmmm...odd.*

"Oh yes, well, I see that." Dr. Corgi paused for a moment. The woman just stood, letting her take in the scene and made no motion to lift the puppy.

Then the owner added, "This is his favorite spot." She looked up and smiled proudly again. No motion to get the pup on the table. *Uhhh, awkward.*

"Oh, well okay, maybe you could lift him out of that, err, cozy place."

"Sure, dear!" replied the owner, giddy with excitement.

With that, she reached deep within her own cleavage and lifted out the little Chihuahua.

Many thoughts came to Dr. Corgi's mind as she first observed this little guy, "Rhett Butler." One of the first, the professional thought, was how horrible this poor little Chihuahua's scabby skin was. The pup had multiple bare spots along its body and down its legs. It had sores from where it had excoriated and chewed on itself. It started to scratch as soon as it hit the table. So the severity was an instant thought, but also, of course, a distracting thought...*How could anybody take something covered in skin issues and place it in between their breasts?* (Side girl thought).

"Well, ma'am, he's got some serious skin disease going on. I believe we should take your little baby and do a skin scrape, a simple test to look for a skin parasite among other things." She then offered a cost and why it was important.

"Well, okay, ma'am," said the owner; she was polite.

Dr. Corgi slowly started to leave the room with the puppy in her clothed arm nook, trying to recover some in her brain, when the women interrupted her. She was mostly out the door to the treatment area, but she looked back.

"Ma'am, I mean, Doctor, is what you're looking for contagious to us people folk?"

"Yes, ma'am, the main parasite I am suspicious of, Sarcoptic mange, is contagious to people."

"Because I have a rash—" And in the blink of an eye, she lifted her shirt, and popped out both of her size triple E bare breasts (complete with pimply rash).

(Insert Dr. Corgi with open eyed-stare and internal scream here.)

Silence. Dr. Corgi had to force her vocal cords into an audible response.

"Aнн, umm, I'm not sure, I'm not a physician. You should contact your doctor, I mean, a human doctor."

"Oh well, thanks, dear. I was just curious," said the owner matter-of-factly, as she covered herself back up.

"Uh, sure."

Step out, close door, deep breath, out of room—*Good job*—and recover.

Yes, the Chihuahua, Rhett, had sarcoptic mange, confirmed. He was treated. This concerned owner was advised that the cozy carrying location may not be a good idea.

Rookie Mistakes

I am always ready to learn although I do
not always like being a taught.

—Winston Churchill

R ookies make mistakes. I think they are unavoidable. Poor Joey
and Nancy, plus Layla, the resident vet tech, had to pay for one
of mine something awful one day. In order to tell you about this
story, I have to tell you about two common treatments in veterinary
medicine.

Thirteen years ago in my rural practice, I followed the sedative
and anesthesia protocols my boss, Dr. Grey Quarter, had in place. He
liked to sedate with a drug called Xylazine. We used to use it a lot,
especially for horses. It has a nice drug that counteracts the effect (a
reversal agent), and the animals wake up really fast. When you give
this sedative, one occasional and not-so-great side effect is that the
animal will throw up. Today, it has been replaced by a more upgraded
sedative, but close relative, Dexdomitor.

Toxiban is activated charcoal. It is used because it binds with
toxic compounds and drugs. It is indicated for any ingestion of things
that might hurt the animal. If the toxin exposure was recent and was
witnessed, the usual protocol is to make the animal throw up. We
have multiple ways to do this, usually peroxide orally or a conjunctiva pill that we place it in the eye; it's neat. If peroxide was used,
the stomach will calm down from expelling the peroxide after thirty
minutes or so. If the eye pill was used and vomiting was achieved,
we just wash out the pill after vomiting is sufficient with eye flush,
and the pill stops working and the pet stops vomiting. Usually at
this point, we can look at the stomach contents and, hopefully, we

see what we were worried about. This usually includes owner's ibuprofen, heart medication, baker's chocolate, rat poison, ant bait, etc. Hopefully, we know what the pet gobbled up, and we see it. To be safe after all vomiting is achieved, it is time to give Toxiban. It takes a lot volumewise, a bowl full most days. It is thick, black, and sugary, but the animals don't seem to mind. They usually lick it right up. Most of the time we put it in a big syringe, and a vet assistant slowly gives it orally to the patient. Over the years, I have had a Labrador or two that I just set the bowl on the floor, and it went ahead and licked up the entire treatment.

I was presented a case of a puppy that had had terrible diarrhea for several days. He was moderately dehydrated. He lay pitifully on the exam table. I did my physical exam. He had had all his puppy vaccines, as I recall. I quizzed the owner about what could be wrong. She had no idea, but she said the puppy does run free about the neighborhood. This, unfortunately, makes a list of potential diagnoses very long. He was negative for parvo, a nasty puppy virus, and negative for parasites. I asked her if I could keep him and give him some IV fluids, gastrointestinal medicine, and some Toxiban since a toxin could be possible. I was trying to cover all my bases. I did not have making him throw up on my agenda because whatever the puppy had eaten or gotten into theoretically was probably several days ago.

We took X-rays, we ran blood work, and I ran in and out of rooms, seeing other cases. The staff asked how much Toxiban I wanted, and I told them. Despite it being a lot, they administered it; they said the puppy was no trouble. X-rays looked okay. Blood work looked unremarkable.

About forty-five minutes later, I had finished the morning appointments and was ready to put an IV catheter in this little fellow. However, this puppy had perked up and wanted no part of this. The two holders could not keep him still. He had come to life, but he was still in need of fluids. If I even went near his leg with the little catheter, he was not having it. He was totally stressed, and this was not what I wanted for him.

Dr. Quarter walked by, glanced at our scene, and said, "Man, what are you doing? That little guy needs a sedative! That's what I would do! If it's the middle-of-the-night emergency and I have no holder, I just sedate 'em." He continued walking and went out to the equine treatment area.

Sure, that will save all this stress! I gave the fella a mild sedative, the Xylazine. The one I mentioned earlier. He started to relax nicely while Joey was holding him. Good.

That's when it all started.

Projectile.

Vomiting.

A horrible turbulent stream of black vomit erupted violently from this otherwise nice-looking little puppy.

It seemed endless, but actually, it was only a few times, just enough to paint the staff in black charcoal syrup.

He vomited the Toxiban. The thick syrup seemed like it was everywhere and on everyone. It was all over the treatment cabinets and dripping behind the doors. After two or three stomach purges, he was finished.

He was sleepy, but he started wagging his tail.

Ugh; obviously, as his doctor, I had forgotten about the Toxiban.

I started to apologize, but it was not enough. Joey, Nancy, and Layla stared, stunned and painted in black vomit.

My ceaseless apologies continued. They all just looked so bad. It was on their clothes. It was on their faces. None of it was on me.

"I'm really sorry you guys" (totally feeling awful).

"Uh, I guess we will need a cleanup," Joe said as he wiped some black sludge off his face.

Then he looked back. "You owe us for that one, Dr. June."

I put an IV catheter in my patient and reversed his sedative.

A little while later, he licked up the Toxiban again, and this time, it stayed in. He did respond well to his therapy.

Everyone in the clinic, despite me saying I would do it, participated in the cleanup. Pizza was ordered for the lunch. Sorry, everyone, I was so pitifully aware that I was a rookie.

The Mayday Bars

"I t's pretty bad, Doctor!"

That was the first thing I heard from Mr. Mack, the worried man with the gruff voice on the phone. He said his little dog, Rocky, was vomiting and had diarrhea. After prompting Mr. Mack with a few questions, he told me Rocky's stool was black, a bad sign of GI ulcers. I became really concerned, and I told Mr. Mack I would meet him at the clinic right away.

When I pulled into the clinic parking lot, a massive eighteen-wheeler was parked there, and a tough-looking middle-aged man was holding a Chihuahua and standing by the clinic's front door. He stood six feet tall and was broad shouldered and a bit round in the middle. He wore a tattered T-shirt, a thick pair of black boots, and worn jeans. A tall, rough type, he may have intimidated me most days, but as I took in his appearance, I also saw the anxiety on his face. I knew it instantly. It was the classic expression of pure worry, no doubt for the little tan dog he nervously stroked.

Over my years of vet practice, I have come to learn that the human-animal bond can immediately break down walls between two people from very different walks of life. I greeted Mr. Mack, and he immediately thanked me for coming into the clinic to help Rocky. I told him, with as much reassurance as I could, it was no problem. We chatted for a moment. He was a trucker with his wife, a common and noble vocation in this town. Nicefolksville (not its actual name, but a more accurate description than the real thing) is a beautiful small town between two major Southern cities. There is a main strip with a Walmart and a half-dozen used-car dealerships. A lot of truckers call Nicefolksville home, so it was not uncommon to see their large vehicles parked in front of an otherwise quiet home in the neighborhood.

When I was on call in Nicefolksville on weekends, my new husband, Marshall, would often come with me. He is not a medical person in any way; he's a military sailor. He is always glad to lend a hand and often finds the unique characters we help on clinic calls very interesting. This visit proved to be the most interesting, even to this day.

Marshall offered to wait with the man at the clinic's front door while I went around back, disengaged the alarms, and turned on the lights. I returned to the front and escorted Mr. Mack and Rocky into a room. When I left to look for my stethoscope, Marshall followed me. I noticed his stunned look. Once out of earshot, he whispered, "You need to ask this guy what he feeds his dog." He glanced at me hard so I could read his expression—appalled and/or nauseated is the only way to describe it. This is uncharacteristic of Marshall, who is usually fazed by nothing. He always finds the sarcastic fun in anything outrageous, but on that particular night, he had not yet fully processed whatever shocking tidbit he was urging me to uncover.

I smiled and responded, "Oh yeah? What did he tell you?" I had heard and seen a lot in my work as a vet already, and I assumed Marshall was overreacting even though it would be unusual for him.

"I can't even go into it." He was serious. Again, it was odd, but I just chuckled at him—must be his lack of dealing with the craziness of the public and their sometimes-misguided pet care.

"Umm. Okay." I smiled at him and thought to myself, I am sure it won't be THAT out of the ordinary for me to hear. I'm much more experienced than he was!

I walked back into the room.

"Hello, sir, so what's going on with poor little Rocky?"

Mr. Mack began to describe the past few days of periodic vomiting. He said Rocky, a one-year-old Chihuahua, had diarrhea, and it had turned black. This is an indication that the small intestine is ulcerated and bleeding, the color of the stool caused by digested blood; the medical term is melena. It is always a dangerous event. The smaller the animal, the faster diarrhea and vomiting can lead to dehydration, often without the owners even realizing it. I proceeded to ask Mr. Mack about possible toxins.

"No," he said. "He just rides in the truck with me. He's with me and my wife, truckin' all the time. He's very important to us."

"Okay, well, what dog food do you feed?" I had begun to suspect that people food might be the problem. It's one of the most common causes of vomiting and diarrhea in animals. I always get this feeling when people talk about their pet like they are a part of the family. They are treated as humans in the family, with bountiful plates of human food and their own seat right at the table. In addition, a complicating factor is that most folks who think this way do not want to admit it to a vet. I resort to baiting them with questions like "What brand of dog food do you feed?" (They don't buy it.) "Is it possible he got a bite of people food?" (Every day, he eats people food.)

Sometimes I have to work for a long period to get it out of them. Some owners, so self-assured, have no problem with plain honesty: "He just eats what we eat."

Giving people food to pets always makes my job challenging due to the serious illness that often results, but I do like an honest owner. It simplifies what can be a frustrating wild goose chase for the cause of the problem. Many veterinarians joke that over time, we acquire necessary mind-reading skills. Early admissions allow me to quickly move on to proper treatment and education. Thankfully, Mr. Mack was one of the straightforward types: "We don't feed dog food, just people food, always."

We were getting somewhere, but I was not ready for what followed.

"Um, okay, sir. That's not good. That tends to cause a lot of problems." Remembering Marshall's warning, I asked more specifically, "What exactly DO you feed him?"

"He eats what we eat, but his favorite thing every day is Payday bars."

Wow, I'd never heard that choice for feeding dogs! That's really awful. Think of the fat and salt content.

I conjured up my most professional manner of speaking.

"Payday bars? That's actually not very good for a dog due to…"
I could see Marshall watching me process this information, like he

knew someone was about to hit me in the face with a pie. Before I could really process any more of Marshall's facial expressions, Mr. Mack interrupted my important line of client education.

"Oh no, no, no, honey!" he said in a reassuring tone. "Don't you worry. It's okay, I mean my wife, ya' see, she chews the Payday bars for him, every bite. Then she spits it out onto the little plate we have for him, and he eats all his food that way all the time. We chew it for him and spit it out. Every bite. Every day. So it's fine."

As a human, I had a moment where my brain stalled. As a new vet, I felt unprepared.

Did they think this would improve digestion? Prevent choking maybe? I mean what? EVERY BITE? EVERY DAY?

Mayday! Mayday! Mayday!

Blank stare. Me, joining my husband. Mouth open. Formulating a response.

Nothing.

Must stop blank stare and commence speaking.

"Uh."

Must do better.

My sarcastic husband, who had recovered before me, having had longer to process this information, looked at me with a raised eyebrow and a smirk as if to say, "Okay, Doc, now what?" Clearly, he was amused by the shock quality of Mr. Mack's statement and my reaction. Then as a bonus, he could observe how long it took me to respond. To him, this scored high in entertainment value.

I tried not to look at Marshall for fear that I would lose my focus and inadvertently break down in nervous laughter at this very concerned and serious owner. I recovered my focus in nutrition. Nutrition. Start there.

I counseled my trucker friend on proper diet. Chewing food for the pet does not substitute for easy digestion, nor can it be considered good nutrition. The high-fat and high-salt foods in this Chihuahua's diet had resulted in a very inflamed GI tract, which caused him to develop very dangerous ulcers. Mr. Mack listened. I cannot always get these people—food-feeding owners—to listen to my counsel, but I could tell that Mr. Mack loved Rocky and did not want the little dog's symptoms to return. He listened intently with his massive shoulders hung low, nodding his head with all of my explanations, and cradling his best canine bud in his arms.

Mr. Mack sighed. "What about steak bits? He likes that too."

"No, sir, that also probably contributed to his problems today."

He accepted what I said and then looked me in the eye. "I will feed what you recommend." He said that he would tell his wife what I said. Then he halfheartedly added that it was really her idea in the first place to feed Rocky that way.

Sure.

I treated Rocky with fluid and ulcer medications, prescribed a bland diet and antibiotics, and the small, friendly dog responded well.

Later in the day, while having a long talk with Mrs. Mack, I went through all of my nutrition recommendations with her. She began, "Well, he likes those Payday bars, and you're sayin' that they're bad for him?" Her deep Southern tone went a bit defensive. "Ya know, ma'am, we picked the candy bar without the chocolate because we knew the chocolate was bad for dogs. We just figured if his food was chewed, it would be okay. His mouth is so small we just wanted him to have an easier time chewing. He's just a little fella. We figured it would be easier for his little tummy to process."

Deep sigh from the missus.

I suspect Rocky still will get a bite of Mom and Dad's food at times, despite my concern and counseling, but it's up to the owner to follow through. My job is to be there for all animal concerns. In the meantime, I always have a moment of joy when unscripted craziness comes across my path.

She Looks Like a Basketball

This story begins with the odd statement being from the owner. We were having a fairly normal day at the clinic. (Never say that.) My receptionist, Sally, a Southerner through and through, was greeted at the front counter by a breeder type who lived down the road. We hadn't seen him in a while. He had a little dog wrapped in a towel tucked under his arm.

"I have a drop-off here, needs a C-section."

Sally stared open mouth. "Well, would you like to talk to the doctor?"

"No, I know the price," said the breeder. He set her on the receptionist's counter like a drop-off package.

"I just want to drop 'er off, I got stuff to do." Sally asked a few more questions, said Dr. June would call him. He said fine.

"Uh, okay. Sign here."

Now, I had to go to C-section often in the country practice. It is a fun procedure to get all the puppies out. While you are sewing the momma dog back up, you can hear all their little puppy voices crying, newborn puppies, a beautiful sign of life. It is my favorite surgery, and I miss it sometimes. Usually, the whole staff is involved, making sure each little puppy is getting dry and warm and has a clear airway. It's a team effort, which makes it even more fun.

The people, however, are usually wishing they had just spayed the pet. In the rural areas, it is usually more common to see this surgery because of the lack of spaying and neutering than it is for reasons of breeding. I did this procedure a lot; one day, I even did it twice. Since I have lived in suburbia now for some time, I have not had a C-section case present to me in ten years—no joke. There is usually a process, check-in, examine, X-rays, blood work, Oxytocin, estimate, etc. Oxytocin is a uterine contraction medication. Sometimes, it is all you need, and you don't have to go to surgery.

But then there was this case.

I can only describe this little momma dog in one way: The way Sally described her as she came busting through the doors into the treatment area.

"Oh my gosh, look at this dog. Mr. Scotty just dropped her off for a C-section. She looks like a basketball!"

I was already in surgery, sewing something up.

I looked up thinking that was so odd—drop-off for a C-section? Then I saw her, a Chihuahua—bless her heart—Mable. She was enormous, her abdomen exactly like a basketball. She looked like a Looney Toons cartoon character that had swallowed a balloon, or a puffed-out puffer fish with little tiny fins. Her little legs were so small and skinny. Her little head was tiny and sweet, with endearing and needy eyes.

She looked at us with quiet desperation. It was like she was saying, "Please help me."

Oh my goodness.

Sally patted her tummy and said, "You poor little momma."

I finished my procedure and walked out into the treatment area. She was wrapped in a little towel, but she still looked like, well, a basketball. Sally had asked how long she has been trying to have puppies. Twelve to twenty-four hours, if I recall, way too long. Normal time is one hour between puppies.

We took an X-ray. There were eight puppies in this tiny dog. On a normal day, without pregnancy, she probably would've only weight eight or nine pounds. Dogs this size may have litters of three or four, but not eight. As I recall, I did my normal work-up, but due to concerns for exhaustion and rupture, I just decided to go to surgery. We called Mr. Scotty; he approved. He stated, "Oh yeah, I thought so."

Hmm, yes.

Eight puppies came out. The staff had fun rubbing all until they started to liven up and administering neonatal care. We allowed Mable, after she was good and awake from surgery, to nurse the puppies. Mable seemed to have a quiet happiness after all that. A happy mom—or maybe just extreme RELIEF.

No Ginger for the Whiskey

I was recently married and still working for the people in Nicefolksville, in my first year of practice. My husband had just received orders to go to the military, and he was very excited. He was so excited, in fact, and since he was prematurely balding, he decided that he would do the shave-all-over, totally bald. So ridiculous, I would tell him. Plus, it was February, and now his head was always cold. Nonetheless, Marshall was excited to begin his career. I just shook my head—he didn't actually have to leave for training for four weeks.

How does this relate? I will tell you, I promise. As I was saying, I was still working at my first job. I had had an experience-filled first year, mostly positive, largely stressful. My on-call schedule was basically seven days on and seven days off.

Often, when I had a night call, my new husband would come with me to help and hold the animals and oversee my safety. One day, it was him and me that were made to feel like we were the oddities.

The call was from the Amish community, and my husband was free, so we decided to go together. This is my second case with them, and I will end up lovingly writing about every encounter.

Lame horses were the problem. The Amish felt they might have laminitis or founder, and they had left a message that the horses were not getting better. Now, the scary part of this is wondering what they had already been treated with. My boss had told me once he went to a colic call and the Amish had placed a six-inch onion rectally in this horse to help it. Ouch. I heard another tale or two about how they give beer to make their horse's kidneys work—that was more well-known...for overworked muscles that lock up. So what was I headed into?

Laminitis is a condition in the hoof where the attachments between the outer hoof wall separate from the bone within the hoof. It is horribly painful to the horse. Unfortunately, if the pain is not alleviated, or the hoof not treated properly, it often can lead to euthanasia as being the only humane option.

We headed out to the farm, me and my bald assistant, in thirty-degree weather. It's cold. We arrive. The farmer is an older, bearded father, maybe in his forties, with a nice Amish farm and several sons. We got out of the vet truck. He looked at my husband, a little scared, probably because of his hairdo or lack of, but the Amish man went ahead and introduced himself. My husband said hello then casually explained that he was not the vet, and he pointed to me. This also took this Amish fella by surprise—an unwanted one—but I had grown accustomed to this, recognizing that I did not have the expected vet look for these parts. We never mentioned to these nice Amish folks that we were romantically together.

The Amish man tried to size me up with a quiet glare. I asked him politely with an attempt at confidence if I could see the horses. He started to walk to a beautiful old barn. As I was walking, I said under my breath, reassuring myself, "Yes, I'm the vet, and I can help horses in pain."

I asked the man what had happened. He said a relative farmer "from the north" came down and started feeding the horses differently, because the distant relative felt that the horses needed double their normal rations. The only reason this relative gave was that his horses up north received twice as much grain, and so the rations should be higher. So they decided to double all the grain rations. Now they could not walk. Founder can be caused by horses being overfed grain. In this case, the horses were not used to it, and they were abruptly doubled. These horses were not thin in any way, and I felt that this is where this farmer had gone wrong. After a careful exam, I confirmed they had founder. They had the telltale throbbing pulses in the fore fetlocks and tenderness at the top of their hooves. The horses were walking like they were on ice or on eggshells, very awkwardly, trying to avoid pain.

I pulled a lot of supplies out of my truck and often was asking my husband to get this and that, but I kept accidentally calling him *honey* instead of his first name. I slowly realized this is why the Amish sons of this man kept jerking their heads to stare at us. I told myself to stop; it was not professional to call your assistant, *honey*, the scary guy with no hair. But then I did it again. *Ugh.* They did not know we were together. They stared again. I debated if I should mention it. I, the five-foot, five-inch female vet, with long hair and my assistant, a bald guy I kept calling *honey.* Maybe this would not be my best first impression. I got distracted and never went back to that thought.

Oh well, I am sure they had some fun discussions about us later on.

The Amish farmer could not afford a lot, like X-rays, so he asked me to just treat them with my medicine. I gave them some treatments. The horses, after some pain injections, seemed greatly relieved. They went from walking on pins and needles to relaxed and calm. I love a horse when it sighs relief after you treat it with pain meds, as I have mentioned before.

They walked more normally into their stalls. I felt I had done well. In addition, I felt that the Amish father and his sons noticed. They were all nodding in approval. I went over the plan for long-term care and feeding rations with the owner. I felt I was doing better, making a better professional impression to what were probably very tough critics. They would eventually tell me the horses made a good recovery. The older man thanked me and walked me back toward my truck.

The atmosphere and tone of his conversation, for a moment, seemed to make me feel respected. I was a little glad he seemed more at ease with his veterinarian for the day.

He started to tell me he knew the real reason he had not been able to fix the horses from the laminitis. I instantly became nervous, but I wanted to seem nonchalant and not insult him in any way. I was super anxious about what type of treatment he would describe, silently hoping it had nothing to do with onions. He said, unfortunately, he did not have what he needed to treat the horses.

I awkwardly asked, "Beer?" I said, trying to hint that maybe I knew something about Amish medicinals. (But really, I don't, of course.)

"No, no." He haughtily chuckled at me. "You use whiskey for laminitis!"

"Oh," I said, bewildered. I asked nervously, "So, you didn't have any whiskey?"

"Oh no," he said. "I *have* whiskey. I gave it to the horses, daily, in fact. They took it well, but it didn't work." Then he added in a strong elder's tone, "The trick is, you need to put ginger in the whiskey, and I had **no** ginger."

Oh, sure.

The Receptionist Is Trapped

The receptionist in a veterinary clinic is a very important position. Sally was our main receptionist. All the clients knew her name. She was a perfect, friendly person for this job. She would become and remains a most treasured friend.

Often, that front desk person's smile is the first a worried pet owner will see or talk to, and it is so important to be positive, compassionate, and friendly. My mother, during my childhood, always knew the name of the front receptionist at the clinics where she took her dogs. She would call them, even if it had been months, and speak easily about what was troubling her in home life and in pet health before she would ever make the appointment. The front staff and the vet were like a trusted family.

Sally was young, in her late twenties. She had taken over the position at our clinic from someone who had been there at the front desk for twenty years, Glenda. She had big shoes to fill, kinda like me, but she also had a big charming smile and a lifelong Southerner's disposition. She was outgoing and friendly with a joyous enthusiasm that seemed to beam out of her. Often, she would get asked about Glenda, but she would charmingly tell everyone that she had retired; people would express their disappointment. Sally took it well, but it did bother her a little. She knew many of the local folks; she had married her high school sweetheart, and they had purchased twenty-five acres as twenty-five-year-olds several years before.

Although Sally was new, the clients really liked her. They saw her as one of their own and felt comfortable venting all their craziness to her. Daily, or hourly, she would get a call that sounded outrageous. Sometimes, the crazy calls were so crazy she couldn't tell if it was real or if Joe was pulling a prank, e.g., "Ma'am, I found a squirrel, it appears to be in labor. How do I help it deliver?"

83

Unfortunately, she always had to be professional. Occasionally, she would get a snickering member of our clinic team on the other end of the line.

She would be there to help me through my most mindboggling, overwhelming situation ever...haunts me still..."Honey, there's a tick on your back."

We just won't talk about that.

Anyway, one day, Sally was going about her day. She was putting people in the rooms for appointments. I could hear her laughing and giggling with her normal exchanges with the country folk. "Oh yeah, wuz yer hound runnin' down in that holler? Bunch of them coon hounds got sick down there."

"Oh hello, ma'am, how are ya'll today? So good to see you, What's troublin' your li'l critters?"

Sally was so full of Southern hospitality, you could not help but feel like you were in her neighborhood, her friendship circles, and her family.

She greeted an older lady in the waiting room that she had dealt with twice before. The lady had a Chihuahua, Prince, with a broken toenail. The Chihuahua did not look pleased to be at the vet, but Chihuahuas seldom do. Ms. Griffon was an elderly lady with a large frame, dressed in straight pants and a V-neck cotton shirt. Ms. Griffon was super concerned, and she told Sally all about how Prince was not putting his foot down, and it was tender.

"Poor little feller!" Sally replied considerately, then added, "Well, all right, let's get 'em in an exam room so the doc can fix 'em up!"

The two walked back to the exam room. Sally opened the door for Ms. Griffon to politely let her in the exam room. As Ms. Griffon was passing her, Sally noticed a big tag on Ms. Griffon, attached to the back of her shirt.

"Ms. Griffon," she said in a very friendly and personable way, and in a whisper, "I believe your shirt is on backwards." Sally offered her best "girl-to-girl" smile.

Ms. Griffon looked and whispered back kindly, "Oh well, I believe you're right dear."

And with that, Ms. Griffon put down her dog and pulled off her shirt.

Yes, she did—right then and there. Sally got pinned behind the exam table with a shirtless seventy-year-old woman, giant brasserie and all. She tried to dart her eyes away and hide, but alas, she could not. The exam rooms were not the large variety.

All Sally could do was stand uncomfortably, holding a record. Ms. Griffon in her underwear slowly examined her inside-out shirt. At a snail's pace, she turned it back to normal. She carefully pulled it on back over head, patted it down a few times. Then she asked Sally how she looked.

Sally, who was still stunned by this client flashing her, said, "Uh, fine." Then she grabbed the door and swung out of the room. Ms. Griffon stood in the room, picked up her Chihuahua, and waited for the doctor.

I saw Sally just a moment later. Her eyes were wide. She looked at me, ran over. "This woman in this room just pulled her shirt off and flashed me, giant bra and everything!

"I barely know her. I just happened to tell her that her shirt was on backwards!" I smiled at Sally. She was and is such a fun person. However, she seemed pretty exasperated. I tried to encourage her. "Well, I guess the clients are really starting to feel at home around you!"

The Number 2 Client:
A Different Kind of Story

D r. Quarter walked into the treatment area with the clinic manager and told us who our top-paying clients were for the year. Ms. Shelly Black had acquired the number one position. She was a bit of a pain, an eclectic breeder who had, as part of a midlife crisis, purchased a large number of purebred dogs and showed up randomly at the hospital for any wide variety reasons. On one occasion, she was also inebriated. She did whatever we recommended, but she was far from appealing to deal with. Plus, she seemed to be developing an obsession for acquiring more and more dogs. The entire staff was always wondering if we should have an intervention with Ms. Black.

The number two client of the clinic was a different sort entirely; it was the Humane Society of Nicefolksville. They called at least once every weekend that I was on call. They knew I had a soft spot for their cause. I could never say no. They were a group of about ten to fifteen dedicated people who were devoted to the care of stray animals. They believed in foster care and rescue, and their lot of animals in need never ever ran dry. They paid $150 for every case to be fixed up. In the country, that purchased you a lot of medicine.

Thank you for your dedication and hard work. It is what I remember, and it inspires me still. Looking back, they were my favorite cases, my **best** victories.

Scariest Patient Ever—Kiwi

He was dropped off, or rather, turned in—cannot pay for services. My vet tech, Layla, said she was willing to try, as she met the patient's former owner in the lobby. They felt bad for the little thing but said, "Can we just give her to you?" Layla, a bit of an animal collector and a newly licensed vet tech, shrugged her shoulders, noticing immediately what the obvious problem with the patient was.

She accepted this offer, knowing that I, Dr. June French, was helplessly unaware in the back treatment area of her decision to treat this animal. Layla knew that I would probably be mildly reluctant but eventually be accepting of delivering medical care. I have the problem of **never** being unwilling to treat any animal in need, even though I said things like, "No, nothing with feathers, scales might be considered, but ultimately must have fur!"

But alas, this patient had feathers. She could have only weighed thirty grams. She was a bright green parakeet with a yellow face and red marks near his eyes. Her name was Kiwi, and she has my title of scariest patient ever. Layla brought her back, wrapped gently in a towel. She said, "I just adopted this guy in the lobby. I want you to try and fix him."

"What?! It's a parakeet!"

"Yes," she said, matter-of-factly. "And it has a broken leg."

She smiled at me, excited over her and, supposedly my, "new project."

"What?! Are you crazy?!" I exclaimed. Layla remained unfazed and positive and basically just ignored me.

I looked at its left leg, clearly broken, with an open fracture no less. An open fracture is a broken leg where the skin is broken and bone is visible. A closed fracture is a broken leg that has skin still intact and is far better from a prognosis angle, since the risk of infection is lower. Layla said, "Oh, but Dr. June, you can fix her, she can be your next success story!"

What? I do not need a project. I am a brand-new vet. Every day, I feel like I am treading water in the deep seas. I was not bored in any way…whatsoever. Ugh…and it's a bird!

I told Layla that I was not a bird vet. She said, "But you know you're all she's got, you should at least look at her, I mean you have all those books…from vet school."

Scowl…Sigh…She got me.

Okay.

I did feel slightly challenged. I do have some friends who are really into birds. I could call them. I have my vet books. Poor little thing must be miserable.

Concerned, I told Layla I wasn't really sure how to even hold the little thing. She said it was easy. "Just do like me." The little bird was wrapped in a small towel.

Gently, so gently so as not to obstruct any airway or cause the animal undue stress, I took the little bird from her. It was a pretty little thing. The green color was vivid and beautiful. Its eyes were wide. It seemed scared, like it did not get handled very often. I slowly began to feel purpose that maybe we could aid this little creature, and it would be exciting.

I gently, gently pulled back the towel to visualize the break in the leg. As I did this, I evidently created a small window of opportunity for this little bird named Kiwi to release all its pent-up anguish over its broken leg.

It wanted someone to blame, I think. It wanted revenge. Its pain scale that it was quietly tolerating was probably a 10 on a scale of 1 to 10, and it needed a way to scream, much like the day I dropped a six-foot oxygen tank on my foot. Yes, that hurt, I broke my toe bone.

This small chance to communicate with me, the holder, was not to be missed. The holder had to know the extent of the anguish. I had allowed one of my fingers, my pointer finger, to creep up near the beak, away from the towel, as we had just started to uncover the leg, so I could look up close.

Kiwi bit down into my finger to the bone and ripped back and forth.

I held on to her but yelled for Layla to help me out. Layla tried every which way to pry her little beak from my fingertip, which now was shredded. Kiwi continued to rip back and forth.

I could not speak in sentences, even if I wanted to. It hurt so bad, I just wanted to throw up. I began to get hot all over.

She stuck a popsicle stick in Kiwi's mouth and a hemostat to see if she could unclench my skin from Kiwi's prongs, but no luck. Kiwi hung on. Her beak was like a master lock embedded in my flesh. This went on with me yowling and trying to be patient with this tiny creature. Nothing seemed to work to make her let go. Then finally, she released and bit into the popsicle stick. It seemed like an hour or two, but it was probably only two minutes, still too long.

It was long enough to kill any desire to pursue any advancement in avian medicine. I will take the racehorse stallion, the feral cat, or the wise and unwilling Chihuahua presented for a nail trim over this bird. Thank you.

Once I became unattached, I tended to my wounds, which were pitifully painful. I was now missing a fingertip, all be it just the fingerprint part. I sat in front of a garbage bin for a few minutes just in case I did vomit.

After some recovery time, I opened my books and followed them like a recipe. I gave Kiwi a shot of butorphanol (diluted), a pain medication. I also created an anesthesia face mask for her so that she could receive the Isoflurane gas anesthesia. This all worked. She became sedated, her little eyes became sleepy. I was so joyous for this.

We had been ready at the start of her procedure. We pulled out the popsicle stick. We cleaned and bandaged her leg and applied our tongue-depressor/popsicle-stick splint. We made her a makeshift super small Elizabethan collar (the lampshade otherwise known as "cone of shame"). I placed on an antibiotic called Baytril. She did fine, as far as I can recall. Her leg didn't heal perfectly, but she had a good quality of life.

Since this day, I have managed limited interactions with parakeets.

Toenails Too Long for Shoes

Winter had come to Nicefolksville. We were deep into February. One day, Dr. Quarter asked me if I would go out to a farm that was quite a ways out. He said that a mare had aborted a foal very early in her pregnancy, but now, apparently, she could not get up. He had some business to attend to at the clinic, but he suggested I take Joe, especially since the roads were unfamiliar to me.

Joe and I hopped in the vet truck and headed out. We headed down state routes until we got to a practically unmarked dirt road. We traveled thirty minutes, making several turns on to various other dirt roads. Country folks often don't have the luxury of a street sign. They must label their roads based on something other than trees and fields, which can be a bit challenging.

Directions:

State route 18, turn right on dirt road behind McKelley's BBQ. Go four miles then turn right at white post. At the fork in the road, veer left. You should see a trailer painted purple with a doghouse. Keep going two miles. Cross bridge over creek (single-car only). Turn right at a row of mailboxes, go one mile. You will see eight trailers on the left and a big field on the right.

Joe laughed at me as with every turn, I was increasingly apprehensive at what was going to happen when I got to where I was going. He just shook his head and smiled as we approached the row of trailers.

"Whelp, we're in the country now!" he chuckled.

I did not chuckle.

I got out. I immediately saw a downed paint mare in the field. A paint mare is a mare with large colored patches, usually brown and white, all over her.

As I had eluded to, it was mid-February and twenty degrees in Nicefolksville. A man approached the vet truck. He was at least six feet, six inches tall, with long gray hair and a long gray beard. He had on overalls and NO shirt underneath. He had a huge hairy chest for all to see. He also appeared to be wearing flip-flops. I was stunned a little since I was next to frozen. He walked forward, reached his hand out to Joe, and introduced himself. Now Joe is twenty years old, but he looked from me to him. "Who is the vet here?" Joey smiled and pointed to me. He walked up to me and introduced himself. "Hey there. Welcome to the country! I am Jimmy Mammoth, and we're glad you're here."

Well, daunting character, but very friendly, at least.

I asked him if maybe he was cold. He laughed. "Not at all," he responded in a booming voice.

Well, okay then.

He opened the gate for us, and we drove into the field, next to the horse. Pear was her name, and she looked totally miserable. She was lying sternal in the field, with her head down, nostrils in the dirt.

I ran over to her with my stethoscope. I placed ONE hand on this mare, and what I felt sent a giant cringe through my body right to my inner spine. One, she was soaking wet with sweat. Two, she felt like an icicle. No living thing should feel like that; it was like death.

She was dramatically hypothermic and just sitting in the cold whipping wind of an open pasture, drenched in her own sweat. She was alive, somehow. I cringed in empathy at how completely wretched she must be feeling.

I looked up at the owner and the small crowd of people that had formed along the fence line, my emotions about to go into overdrive.

"Someone! Please get her a blanket! She is frozen!" I hollered, minimally professional.

At my desperate cue, three older women took off from the line up at the fence post. I assumed they were off to find a horse blanket for this poor mare. There were a few other horses nearby, and I figured someone had to have a horse blanket to put on horses. But this was not the horse-show world. I was in the country, or rather what solid country folk would call the boondocks.

Horse blankets come in various sizes and are usually adjustable with buckles under the girth area and around the front of the chest. We used to have piles of them at the stable where I kept my horse as a kid. When I was twelve, I remember it was trendy to buy the Gore-Tex blankets for your horse. It was a million miles away from what I saw when these women came running back to me.

After a further quick exam on poor Pear, I determined her body was going into hypothermic shock, and I ran to my vehicle. I grabbed her some Banamine, a pain medication, and gave it to her right in the vein. I looked at her hind end. She appeared to still have the placenta, or afterbirth, hanging out of her. Mr. Mammoth watched. Joey tried to get her temperature. I tried to figure out if this was just a case of retained placenta or if something had gone wrong when she passed the baby. I ran over to the very premature deceased baby It appeared to be four to five months old, all intact. A full-term foal is born after eleven months of pregnancy. This one was very immature, about the size of a thirty-five-pound dog. As I hurried back to the mare, I passed something on the ground that was curious: a placenta. I picked up a stick and pulled it up. The whole thing was there with a single hole where the baby had poked through, lying on the grass.

I looked at Joe. "If this placenta is to that baby, then…what's that coming out of the mare?"

I had an idea. It was uncommon in horses, but if it happens, it will usually cause mares to lose their pregnancies. Joe shrugged his shoulders and shook his head. I secretly felt mighty astute that I had not missed this.

I suited up with my long gloves. I put my obstetrics hat on so to speak. I think this mare is still in labor, with another foal.

While I did this, the ladies returned running. Their actions would help me realize in the next few moments that all these folks had big hearts.

As the three ladies scurried toward me, they looked like three giant pyramids with legs. Their arms were stuffed full of comforters and homemade quilts, from every bed in their trailers, no doubt. Just a peep of an eyeball looked around the mountain of blankets to see where to go. Across the field they came, gloriously fulfilling their mission.

I smiled but realized in an instant there were no other options for this horse. We took several of the blankets and put them on her neck, shoulders and across her back. After just a minute or two, with the Banamine injection on board, the mare started to relax a bit.

I put a gentle wash on the mare's vaginal area and did my obstetric assessment that this was, in fact, the case. She was trying to pass another premature, undersized baby.

Twinning in horses is a deadly thing. A few weeks after breeding, the mare should be checked by a vet with an ultrasound to assess the pregnancy for twinning. Twinning is rare, but 99.9 percent of the time it will, sadly, cause a miscarriage of the pregnancy. To a hopeful breeder, it is also a loss of the investment in time and money. Sometimes it will cause death of the mother, especially if she makes it to the later stages of pregnancy. Her body was not designed for twins. It's extremely rare for the foals to ever survive. More often than not, once the body is overwhelmed, it miscarries both.

Mr. Mammoth was now standing beside me. I told him as I palpated this little foal inside the mommy what was happening. With each contraction, I would pull. I stared at the ground for concentration; I had so many eyes on me. Big pressure for a definite rookie. That's when I saw a very odd detail.

Mr. Mammoth was wearing flip-flops because his toenails were all three or more inches long. There was no possibility a shoe would fit these feet. I had never seen anything like it. His toenails were silver and gray with rippling layers that made them look like dagger-style oyster shells. They extended out past his sandals, in zig zag curves, and into the frozen grass.

Oh my, what on earth...

I tried to refocus, but it was so distracting since he was right next to me—this man acting like it was the hot summertime when it was not. It was freezing and windy, and he had no shirt on.

Inside my brain went something like this:

*Oh gosh...*trying to concentrate on my task.

Don't look…don't look…nowhere to look, stare at the horse. Stare at your hands, don't look, focus on what you're doing…oh, I looked.

UGH! His toe nails are so long! Why does he have no shirt on?! And seriously, what is wrong with toenail clipping?

Concentrate, the mare is about to push, and we will need to pull… oh, here she goes pull…baby is coming…good!

How do you stand having toenails that long? It would probably just take a minute to cut that—well maybe not, they do look super thick. Hoof trimmers might be needed…ugh, Concentrate!

A moment later Pear stood up, she shook a little. Clearly, she was feeling better. I continued on. She gave a giant heave, and the foal came out feet first. Mr. Mammoth put his bare hands on the little hooves, right next to mine, and waited with me for the next push. Once more, she pushed it all out, this second little baby (which had already passed, poor little fella). The lineup of residents on the fence all began to cheer and holler. The afterbirth in full followed the foal with a final push.

Pear picked up her head, heaved a sigh, and shook her mane. It was the relief sign that I love so much. The trailer park folks began rubbing her dry underneath her sets of comforters. I gave her some antibiotics to help with possible uterine infections from all that trauma. I finished her other treatments. I warned the owner about possible complications.

But Pear did great.

I called Mr. Mammoth a week later, and he sounded so pleased. Pear was a big star in their parts. Everyone could not stop talking about it, and Pear had no complications. He seemed open to my recommendations to wait a few months to try to breed her again. I told him to check her with an ultrasound a few weeks after she's bred. He thanked me kindly.

It has been many years since I was there on that day. Some of the fine details are fuzzy, but I do remember the mare, the women— and the toes.

Calf Pull 1: The Back Forty

I would like to now introduce Drs. Bill and Melissa Braford, who were classmates of mine in vet school. They met in their first year of vet school and were inseparable from that point on.

Mr. Bill Braford, now Dr. Braford, was previously an Army man. He was a bit gruff, opinionated, but well spoken and courteous. He has a good sense of humor and loved to point out the funny sarcasm in all things. Currently, the Brafords own a mixed-animal practice together.

Early in their careers, shortly after being married, they took jobs in the mountains at such a practice. It was a bit rural, but they felt they were ready to begin trying to help all types of animals.

A few weeks into their jobs, the clinic received a call that there was a down cow in the back forty that couldn't deliver her calf. This is a common problem in the world of bovine medicine. The birth canal of the cow is a challenging exit. They teach you about it at length in vet school.

The receptionist took down the directions to a Mr. O'Dell's farm and handed the directions to Dr. Bill Braford. Being new, he asked the receptionist about the roads. She said she wasn't sure about that part of the county, but she said she thought he would be *okay*. She handed him the clinic cell phone and the farmer's number, just in case.

Directions: Take State Road 192 just before county line; turn left onto Huckle Road (dirt). Follow road for a few miles until you get to the Simpson's place; turn left there and go three miles.

Dr. Bill followed the directions and found Huckle Road. He went down Huckle Road and looked for a farmhouse. He kept going down the dirt road that had other dirt roads feeding off every which way, but there were no farms or farmhouses, just open pasture and occasional trees. Finally, after continuing on Huckle Road for a good five miles, he decided something was wrong. He called the farmer from the vet truck's mobile phone.

"Hello, sir, I am the vet, Dr. Bill Braford, and I'm trying to get to your pasture, but I can't find the place you called the Simpson's place."

"You don't know where the Simpson's place is? Everybody knows where that is."

(Awkard pause. Dr. Bill at a momentary loss of words.)

"Well, no, sir, I am not from around here, I'm new new to the area. Can you tell me where it is or what I need to be looking for? I am five miles down Huckle Road."

"Well, you're new, eh? I can't believe you don't know where it is!" replied Farmer O'Dell.

"Well, could you help me? Could you describe it? Maybe I can't see it from the road."

"Well, it's hard to say. There's nothing there right now, cause the Simpson's place burned down twenty years ago."

"Sir, well, I am not sure how I am supposed to find it if it is actually not there anymore."

"Well, I guess that would be a problem. Hmm, there's a big black oak there that got struck by lightning—maybe that's where you should turn."

"Oh, okay," replied Dr. Bill skeptically.

"Still can't believe that, I mean **everybody** knows where the Simpson place is."

Dr. Braford, still shaking his head, backtracked about three miles until he found what appeared to be a large burnt oak. He turned and went three miles. Where he found, in front of a farmhouse, a man in a truck who waved him to follow him out to the "back forty," a reference to acreage.

They entered a large pasture surrounded by rocks and trees. Off to one side was a poor downed momma cow with two feet coming out of the back of her.

Dr. Braford got to work helping this cow. The whole time, Farmer O'Dell was eyeing him uneasily, kinda acting like he is not sure of this not-from-these-parts veterinarian.

Dr. Braford tried to keep his poise and know-how. He spoke frankly.

"This calf is really large! How long has it been stuck?"

"Few days."

Groan.

"How long has she been lying here?"

"Well, a few days, I guess. Back legs won't even move to get up."

Ugh, that's terrible. She might be paralyzed.

The vet put all his strength and calf-pulling skills to work and finally, out came an eighty-five-pound calf, which is particularly large. The smell was terrible. He cleaned up, changed his gloves, and was about to go back in to check the uterus when the owner piped up.

"What are you doing now?" Mr. O'Dell said with a grimace.

"Well, I'm gonna check her for a twin," replied Dr. Bill frankly.

"That's crazy, no cow is gonna have a twin, especially with that giant calf inside of 'em," the farmer said.

That didn't stop Dr. Bill from going into the uterus, and sure enough, there was another eighty-five-pound calf.

He pulled and pulled and finally, after a lot of hard work, got the second calf out. It too was already deceased and decomposing. He reexamined the mother cow.

Mr. O'Dell did not have any words to offer as he could see he had clearly been wrong.

Dr. Bill offered to euthanzie the cow, since she was permanently paralyzed from her ordeal, and he felt that she had been suffering, but on a side note, farmers have a method for this as well. He told Mr. O'Dell, "Either you or I could do it, but it's not okay to let her sit here and suffer, because she is permanently paralyzed from this delivery and from being in labor so long. She cannot walk at all or get up."

Mr. O'Dell exploded in anger. "You better not say such a thing! She'll be fine, she'll be fine! You're horrible! You do not know nothin'!"

"Sir, I am just trying to do what is right for the cow. She is paralyzed, and she shouldn't suffer anymore."

Mr. O'Dell got in Dr. Bill Braford's face, ready for a showdown.

"You look here!" screamed Mr. O'dell, "I knew this was gonna be a problem from the moment you—"

That's when the black blur emerged from behind a rock, with a groan, of sorts. It moved slowly, like it had just awakened. It fumbled about. It was a stone's throw away.

"Mr. O'Dell, get in the truck right now," Dr. Braford whispered.

"No I will not you ——," Mr. O'dell hollered.

"No. Get in the truck right now," a panicking Dr. Braford whispered.

"I will not shoot my cow!" shouted Mr. O'Dell, his red eyes wide.

"Well, it don't matter," said Dr. Braford. "You need to get in the truck before we get eaten by that **black bear** that's just twenty-five yards away right there."

Mr. O'Dell's head flung around to witness the disturbed creature stumbling out of its cave. It was enormous.

"Oh yeah, okay. I'll get in my truck."

The cow was put out of her suffering just a short while later when the back forty appeared to be clear.

Calf Pull 2: Ice-capades

I t was in the middle of a heavy winter. The snow had covered the countryside, and spring was still a month or two away. The temperatures had dropped down to twenty degrees, causing everything to freeze. One of the area's large farm managers called the clinic to report a cow with a stuck calf, and he asked if anyone could please help him because he could not catch this cow. She was a bit ornery—and she was running around in the back forty, evading her pursuers, with calf legs coming out of the back of her. She was a mean Charolais momma.

Dr. Bill Braford was assigned this task. He carried his drug dart gun that was used to sedate. That's what this farm manager was hoping for, since no one could catch the cow.

Dr. Bill met the manager, Steve, at the farm entrance. They had met before.

"Hey there, Steve, long time no see," Dr. Braford said.

"Yeah, hey there, Doc, sorry to call you out in this weather, but, well, this particular cow is tricky. She's not the nicest to deal with, and now she has had a stuck calf for a day or two."

The two took the vet truck out to an enormous rolling pasture. It was all open field, but there was a problem. That open field was a total sheet of ice. The cow was up on top of a hill. The vet truck pulled into the pasture, slowly up on the hill, and stopped. There was a quarter mile between where the vet truck was parked and where the cow was standing. She looked at the two men suspiciously, like in her mind, she was saying, "You can forget it." She stood her ground and gave a defiant snort.

Dr. Bill Braford aimed at his target, with his target looking on. He pulled the trigger.

Boom. The dart hit her right in the back thigh. The cow trotted a bit then stopped. She seemed to stumble some. Steve and Dr. Braford watched, getting ready to act as soon as she lay down and work on her stuck calf.

But she didn't lie down. Instead, she wandered over to the edge of the hill. Both men held their breath. Then much to their dismay, like Bambi on ice, or as if on a sled, the cow slid gracefully on all four hooves, down the steep incline to the bottom. Once she got there, she decided it was okay to lie down, and she fell asleep.

Dr. Braford made his way down the icy slope with his calf-pulling supplies. Steve was right behind him. The doctor listened to the cow's heart and then went to work. He pulled the calf without much trouble—easy, no problem. But always as vets, we must be careful when we think things are going well.

He finished cleaning her up and decided to give the sleeping bovine the sedative reversal agent her when he was finished so she would wake up. He gave half the reversal agent in the vein and the other part of the reversal agent in the muscle so this known-to-be-ornery cow might wake up just a tad slow.

Dr. Braford collected the last of his supplies and started up the hill. Steve had already made it most of the way back up the incline.

That's when he heard it, like a stomping, an unsettling ice crunching noise from behind him. He turned. It was the Charolais. She was awake, upset, and out for vengeance.

Maybe it was the dart in her thigh she did not approve of.

And she was coming right at Dr. Bill. He was probably the last thing she remembered before her sedated slumber. Snorting and stomping but slipping and sliding, she charged right at Dr. Braford. He began frantically climbing the ice hill.

Slipping and struggling, up the hill he went in a fierce undertaking. He expended lots of energy, but does that really matter when your feet are sliding every which way? Luckily, the enraged cow did not appear to have ice talents in her charge and was slipping in her quest to trample Dr. Braford.

Dr. Braford climbed to the top of the slope, where he tried desperately to flag Steve. Then began ice sliding and running to the truck.

"Go! Go!"

"What?! Why?"

"Start the truck...DRIVE...She's coming!" Dr. Braford hollered. "The cow! She's COMING!"

Steve's eyes grew wide in acknowledgement. He ran for the truck as Dr. Braford slid his way across the ice.

The Charolais topped the hill and continued her furious charge.

Steve fired up the truck as the cow kept gaining in on Dr. Braford. Just in the nick of time, the vet leapt onto the back of the vet truck.

"Drive!" yelled Dr. Braford

"What?" Steve yelled back.

"I said DRIVE, you SOB...Drive!"

Steve hit the gas, with Dr. Braford hanging on to the back of the vet box in dramatic fashion. They flew back to the gate of the pasture with the Charolais still in pursuit. Finally, the cow acknowledged her defeat and turned away.

Never a dull moment.

The Nudist Colony

D r. Melissa Braford was in her first few years of practice in the mountains and had gotten to know the area fairly well. The older veterinarian, who was her boss, told her that rumor was, somewhere out there, there was a hidden community of naked people. The staff would occasionally joke about it. Dr. Melissa said it was all ridiculous, since no one at the clinic had ever seen it and had no idea where it was located. But her boss, who knew these woods well, seemed very curious and amused.

"Somewhere in the far west corner of the county, but I don't know, never had a call there," one of her coworkers said.

Just a crazy rumor. (Shaking head.)

Little did she know that she would be the one to unravel this fabled mystery.

Dr. Melissa Braford is a kind and systematic veterinarian. She has a compassionate, secure, level-headed approach to her work. She is, in her private life, a happily married, conservative individual.

On a Sunday around 6:00 p.m., she got a voice message regarding a sick and apparently blind goat. Dr. Melissa didn't recognize the number, but she called it back.

"Hello, did you call for a veterinarian? You have a sick goat?"

"Hello, oh yes, ma'am, my little goat appears to be running into the fence and the trees. He can't make it into the barn without crashing into the poles. It's awful!"

"Have we ever been out for veterinary care to your place before?" Dr. Melissa Braford asked.

"No, ma'am, but I really need some help, and Mr. Kellam gave us your name. He owns the feed store." *Dr. Melissa did recognize this reference.*

"My name is Betsy," the owner said. "And my husband and I live on a small farm, 112 Albare Street."

Dr. Melissa reviewed her cost, asked a few more questions, and said she would be out that way, should be about thirty minutes.

"Dr. Vet, umm, I'll meet you at the gate, 554 Ridgemoore Road, and I'll let you in. I'll be there with my golf cart."

Fine, Dr. Melissa said. She took down the address and headed out in her truck.

Dr. Melissa Braford followed the woman's directions, driving up the road and turning onto the paved and well-marked Ridgemoore Road. There were no marked driveways, just open fields. In the distance, she saw an occasional house, but no people.

Finally, she came to a large gate, and there beside the gate was a normal-looking, conservatively dressed woman in a golf cart. Above the gate hung a sign identifying this as the entrance to a community. It seemed very formal, almost like the entrance to a modest country club.

Dr. Melissa wondered why she'd never known about the community, being that she had practiced in the area for a few years. She stepped out of her vet truck and greeted the nice woman, Betsy.

"Hello, I'm Dr. Melissa Braford."

"Well hello, I'm Betsy! I am so relieved you are here!" she exclaimed.

"No problem, ma'am. Should I follow you?"

"Oh yes, just follow the golf cart. Oh, and by the way, I need to mention that this community is a bit special."

"Oh yeah, how so?" replied Dr. Melissa.

"Well, folks here don't actually wear any clothes. Or, rather, clothes are optional."

Dr. Braford casually nodded her head, but as the statement sunk into her brain, fear tore through her insides.

"Excuse me, what did you say?" Dr. Braford asked again to make sure she heard it right.

"Well, actually, this is a community that is a clothing-optional community. Many people here do not wear any clothes. Are you okay with that?"

Oh dear, I'm here, it's real, I have to drive through this place, how do I do that with my eyes closed...so awkward...can I go home...she asked me a question...

"Um, okay, that's fine," Dr. Braford heard herself saying.

"Don't worry, most folks won't be out and about this time of day!"

"Oh, okay."

Oh my gosh.

She heard two other golf carts passing through a crossroad area ahead, started to glance up, but panicked and forced herself to look down straight down at the ground.

She got back in her vet truck, scared of having to drive through such a community. She stared at the back of the golf cart and started the engine. Forceful staring would be the answer. *Do not take your eyes off the golf cart.* Dr. Melissa Braford knew that at least this one person was dressed.

Off they went through the community. Dr. Melissa, focused intently on the back of the golf cart, made it through multiple turns and a few stop signs. Thankfully, despite a few golf carts going in opposite directions, she arrived without witnessing any bare skin, anywhere.

She reached a small house with a modest barn and fenced-in corral off to the side. Betsy pointed to her male goat that was stumbling about, crying occasionally, and Dr. Melissa was immediately glad that she came. The little goat ran into two or three trees while she watched.

She went out to the goat and started to examine it. It did appear to be blind and wobbly. She asked Betsy about the goat's care, parasite control, possible toxins or trauma. Dr. Melissa then asked what Betsy was feeding the goat.

"Oh, corn and hay," Betsy replied.

Dr. Melissa knew immediately what was wrong, went out to her truck, and pulled up an injection of thiamine, vitamin B1. This goat had polio, or rather Polio encephalomalacia, which causes lesions in the gray matter of the brain. This was set off by a high-carbohydrate, poor-roughage diet that had led to a vitamin deficiency. (The goat did respond well to this treatment and eventually made a full recovery.)

Dr. Melissa educated the owner on proper nutrition. She sat in her vet truck afterward and wrote up the bill for services rendered. She politely handed it to Betsy.

"Oh, let me get my husband. He pays the bills."

As Betsy ran toward her house, Dr. Melissa glanced up. Betsy's husband was standing at the window, bare chested. Only his head and upper half were visible. He had been watching all this veterinary business go down at his place, probably casually in his birthday suit, but no one knows for sure. He watched his wife come in the side door and stepped back.

Dr. Melissa became uneasy; she did not know if these people were defiant in their bare exposure. Betsy was dressed, but what would her husband do?

Betsy came running back out of the house toward the vet truck.

"He's coming. He's gonna write you a check."

Fear crashed over Dr. Melissa Braford.

"Well, maybe he can just mail it in," said Dr. Melissa with a sense of urgency.

But just then the door to the house opened and steps toward the vet truck were heard. Dr. Melissa could not look up—her uneasy stomach was in her throat.

"Oh no, Dr. Braford, he's right here, see. He's got your money."

Dr. Melissa wondered was this to be the most awkward, totally unwanted nudity moment? He was nearby, like next to the truck now, on the passenger side. She could only hope that some form of coverage would be arrayed, or at the very least the vet truck door would help block out private parts. *Ugh.* She hazarded a split-second side glance.

There, standing before her, was a very tall man…wearing a bathrobe.

And holding out a check.

Thank you, Lord! Whew!

She collected her check calmly, like nothing was abnormal at all. She rolled up her window and breathed a sigh of relief. She fired up the vet truck. She had but one final hurdle to jump: she had to survive the exit out. She began her stressful departure from this hidden bare-all community by closely trailing Betsy's golf cart once again. On the way out, she had a few close calls. Some folks tried to wave at Betsy and have a conversation, golf cart to golf cart style, about her goat. However, Betsy graciously waved them on and said, "We'll chat later!" and she motored on. Dr. Melissa had her extreme stare on the back of the golf cart. She saw glimpses of edges of fences and brick buildings in her peripheral vision. Finally, elated, she saw the big gate ahead. The exit.

Betsy opened the gate for her and bid her good-bye and thanked her graciously.

Dr. Melissa Braford exited the "community" and never laid eyes on a nudist, or much of the neighborhood itself, actually.

She did, however, have the honor of confirming this mystery community to her boss, who was a little disappointed he hadn't been the one to take the call.

The Stray Kitty

D r. Melissa Braford was going about her day—not too eventful, but steady. Her husband, Dr. Bill, was out working on farm calls. The receptionist came back and told her that two of her favorite elderly clients were at the front counter. These two ladies had, on occasion, picked up a stray cat and brought it down to the clinic. They had big hearts for kitties, and over the years, they had contributed part of their modest income to have the kitties fixed up and helped on their way into new homes.

The first of the pair, Ms. Evelyn Campbell, was sweet, with white hair pulled into a bun. She had a stature that was slightly bent and stood no more than five feet. She would speak to you with trembling hands, and she was full of stories from the local areas. She would get so excited when she had your attention, telling you a story of how the animal care used to be or about that kitty she saved from long ago. Ms. Margie Rockwell, on the other hand, was quiet and slow and tended just to follow Ms. Campbell around. She walked with a cane and had dark gray hair that was short and curly. She always had good questions about kitty medicine. Together, the pair of kind older ladies would invite anyone to join in their friendly banter, and whoever part took in their presence would become enamored with two lively ladies.

On this day, they stood at the counter, telling the receptionist they had found a stray kitty on the side of the road, and they wrapped it in blankets and put it in the trunk. They explained in dramatic fashion that they were concerned because the kitty didn't look like it could walk very well, so they had caught it themselves and decided to bring it to Dr. Melissa. They were very emotional—this was to be the next great rescue story for years. They told the receptionist, with great confidence, they knew Dr. Melissa could help it.

Ms. Campbell was already telling the tale. "I said, 'Here, kitty, kitty,' and that kitty just looked up. He tried to step toward me, and then he just let me put him in our blanket. Poor kitty!"

Ms. Rockwell nodded at this and told how she just happened to have a large blanket in the back of the car, and the kitty seemed to feel better when they put it on the blanket and laid it in the trunk. They petted him for a while to calm him down, but he could barely move, so they brought him to the vet right away.

Ms. Campbell began with her disappointment in the transportation decision. "I had wanted to just put him in the backseat and talk to him some, but Ms. Rockwell was concerned he would get up and fall more. But I really wanted to pet him for his car trip."

"He did fine in the trunk," Ms. Rockwell said. "He did not move at all, and besides, it's my car." She glared at Ms. Campbell.

They seemed concerned about moving the cat, so they had not brought him inside but didn't want him to wait too long if possible since he was in the trunk of the car. Dr. Melissa Braford wrapped up a case in the back of the treatment area and walked up front to the reception area, where her receptionist filled her in.

"Where did they go?" Dr. Melissa asked her receptionist.

"Oh, they went outside. It's in the trunk of the car, and they're not sure if they should move it or not."

"Oh well, okay."

Dr. Melissa Braford looked out into the parking lot, where a few other families were loading and unloading their pets. One family had a puppy in hand and a baby in a stroller. Then she saw two elderly ladies hunched over the trunk of a Buick. Ms. Rockwell, at that moment, was reaching in the trunk and pulled an animal wrapped in a blanket out of the back of the car and placed it on the sidewalk in front of the vet clinic. It seemed like its head was peeking out through the blanket. Since there was no leash or carrier, Dr. Melissa hollered at her vet assistant to come help and ran out to the parking lot—to hopefully prevent a feral cat from running off. She greeted the ladies and quickly looked down at the patient who was still on the sidewalk but had gone back under the blanket.

"We found him on the side of the road couldn't hardly move, but he let us pick him up," explained Ms. Campbell.

Dr. Melissa pulled back the towel slightly. There was a dull sounding cat growl of sorts. She did a double take. This was not a feral cat at all; it was in fact a juvenile bobcat. Yes. There it was a weakened **bobcat** on the sidewalk, in front of her animal hospital, with lots of family-type people walking their dogs in, and these two elderly ladies had been petting and cuddling it.

"What do you think, Dr. Braford?" Ms. Rockwell asked.

"Uhh, I need some help!"

Dr. Melissa Braford called for help. She told the kennel help to get a dog carrier and some cat gloves. (Cat gloves are huge thick gloves for vet staff to handle less-than-friendly felines.)

"Poor kitty, bless his heart," said Ms. Campbell.

"Ma'am, this is a bobcat!" Dr. Melissa explained, still in a bit of shock.

"A what, dear?" said Ms. Campbell.

Before she could answer, she got the kennel attendant to help her slide the kitty into the carrier. Then once the door was shut, she breathed a sigh of relief and decided to address the capturers.

Dr. Melissa Braford, said once more, with added volume, "It's a BOBCAT."

"Oh my," the ladies gasped.

She explained to the two elderly ladies they had not found a domestic kitty, but in fact a sickly bobcat. The two women looked at each other, and both raised their eyebrows at the same time. They still seemed concerned. Dr. Melissa asked if they had been bitten.

"Oh no, nor scratched," said Ms. Rockwell, with a look of shock.

"Poor sweet little thing, he's sweet," said Ms. Campbell, who seemed unfazed.

"Well, actually, I think he's sick, and you got really lucky he did not bite you!"

"Well, he must've known we were there to help him," said Ms. Campbell, matter of fact.

Ms. Rockwell said nothing, but she did have a look of bewilderment upon her face.

Dr. Melissa's clinic transported the somewhat juvenile feline to a wild-animal rehab center where it did make a full recovery. The wildlife veterinarian felt it might've gotten hit by a car, but it was going to be all right. The bobcat would get released back into the wild eventually.

Dr. Melissa kept Ms. Campbell and Ms. Rockwell informed on the recovery of the bobcat. She also asked the pair of ladies, next time they find an animal, maybe just call the vet on call and they would be happy to come to the location instead of just placing the animal in your trunk.

"Okay, sure," said Ms. Campbell.

"That's a good idea," confirmed Ms. Rockwell.

*Cats...aliens...*Kitty after a pause, asked if perhaps that litter box was placed outdoors and questioned that maybe a raccoon or other wild animal was getting into the litter. Ms. Curl was appalled at this outlandish statement, "My cats NEVER go outdoors!"

She continued. "Also, the aliens have chewed a hole in my floor. The landlord doesn't believe me, but they are eating the house. I can hear them in the walls, and I see them running around."

Kitty Mutt decided the most logical approach was to offer other scurrying-animal scenarios. Hoping this would turn the conversation and make it more normal, "Could there be mice in your new home?"

Ms. Curl paused, then added, "I have NEVER seen anything like this before. Ever. It's not like a rat, or a mouse, or a reptile. It's aliens!"

Carolina Mountain Oysters

D r. Nina Springer looked back—back to her life as a vet student. She pondered on the incidents early on in her training that were similar to those of James Herriot. She was very surprised to find how unpredictable veterinary medicine could be right from the beginning. These beginning experiences confirmed for her that this was an exciting career she was going to love.

Nina was required to get real-world experience by working at a vet practice during her final twelve weeks of the four-year vet school program. Most vet students choose to work at a clinic near their desired location, while others choose exotic places and unique experiences found in places like Ireland and the hunting preserves in South Africa.

Nina chose to work with Dr. Melvin Martin at an equine hospital in the Carolinas. She knew she'd acquire a lot of equine experience there. He was a sweet, short, balding fellow with a deep Southern drawl. Right away, Nina and Dr. Martin hit it off. She soon knew she had made an excellent choice for her veterinary externship.

Each morning, after ensuring that the large white vet truck was well stocked with supplies and, most importantly, with good snacks, Nina would hop in, excited for what the day would bring. Together, Dr. Martin and Nina would roam the Low Country, taking in the swamplands and the many old plantations. Dr. Martin had a vast amount of experience in the area. He knew all the roads well but knew the local restaurants even better. Each day, after the morning appointments, Dr. Martin would enjoy a huge sit-down meal, usually accompanied by copious amounts of biscuits and sweet tea. He would never let the future Dr. Nina Springer pay for anything. She tried her best to keep up with the huge caloric intake of each day. Some of the meals lasted an hour or more. Typically, after lunch, Nina found herself driving the vet truck with Dr. Martin peacefully snoring in the seat beside her.

In the Carolinas, particularly in the Low Country, there is a large population of Gullah people who speak an English-African creole language.

Often you will see Gullah women on the side of a highway, selling their homemade baskets made of sweetgrass, singing softly. Their dialect was very difficult for Nina to understand, but Dr. Martin was accustomed to hearing it and could communicate just fine.

One early afternoon, five Appaloosa stallions were scheduled to be castrated at a Gullah farm. It is unusual for a farm to have that many stallions to castrate at once, but Nina was looking forward to the experience to be gained by the procedures. She had only castrated young colts at that point in her career. Colts are smaller; their castration procedure is faster and is typically performed with the anesthetized animal lying on the ground. Dr. Martin preferred standing castrations for stallions due to their large size. For a standing castration, the horse is given a sedative, and local anesthesia is administered. The local anesthetic drug, which numbs the area, is injected in copious amounts around the scrotum area and injected into each testicle.

Nina applied her skills at equine surgery. Five horses—Dr. Martin training her on each one, proceeding methodically: sedate, inject, cut, clamp and repeat. Part of the method in the procedure is to toss the removed testicle aside and pick it all up at the end of the surgery.

The afternoon was hot and thick with humidity in the Southern sun. Nina wiped her brow and noticed at a side glance one of the Gullah family members had picked up the testicles and threw them in a bucket. Dr. Martin didn't notice this as he was focused on coaching the future Dr. Nina Springer's actions through each surgery. The

Gullah men were hanging around, watching and holding the horses for Nina. They had a lively, sing-song conversation going amongst themselves, very little of which Nina understood. By the third horse, sweat was running in rivers down Nina's back. She had Betadine stains all over her forearms and hundreds of tiny specks of blood on her scrubs. One stallion tried to stomp vigorously at a fly and came down on Nina's toe instead. The task was proving to be quite the challenge.

Finally, the last horse was finished. Nina realized she could barely stand up after bending under the horses so long. She was a bit expired and ready just to get back on the road. Usually, it was Nina's job as part of her externship to review postoperative care with the client. However, Nina could not communicate with the folks, so she let Dr. Martin do all the talking. Finally, the two packed up, and Nina collapsed on the front seat.

A little while later, what seemed like only twenty minutes or so, the phone on the console rang. Nina answered and heard all kinds of unintelligible mumblings going on. She asked the caller to repeat himself, but he handed the phone to someone else with, evidently, the same problem speaking, "I cam feel mah yips," is all she heard, over and over.

She realized it was the probably one of the Gullah family. Nina, embarrassed by her inability to communicate with these folks, just handed the phone to Dr. Martin.

He began chatting, but was instantly alarmed.

He then replied, "You did *what*? You, you—OH NO!—you didn't? Heee-heee HA-HA-HA." Dr. Martin bellowed. He began to turn red and, while in the fits of laughter, was having trouble catching his breath. Nina stared in bewilderment; she still didn't get it. Dr. Martin, in between his spasms of laughter, motioned for Nina to take the phone and talk again to the Gullah folks.

"Tell them—hee-hee-hee—OH MY!" he kept cackling, gasping for air. "Tell them not to eat any more of those stallion balls AND the numbness in their lips should wear off in an hour or so!"

First Encounter of the Camel Kind

After a year of country practice, I had to step out of the country and into the affluent countryside of a very Southern city. I was sad to leave my beloved comrades in Nicefolksville, but my husband had his orders. It was our first military move after Marshall's military OCS training, and with it, I landed right smack in the middle of a very large collection of horse show people, dressage enthusiasts, fox hunters, and pony clubbers. I would soon find out that these groups had their own set of unique challenges.

I asked many of my clinician friends about a good job in the area, and they sent me to Dr. Hank Shire's practice. Dr. Shire had practiced in the horse community for twenty years and was not in need of a full-time vet, but I offered to work part-time, and he accepted if I agreed to go on call every third weekend. That was still a step up from my previous job (seven days on/seven days off), and I figured I would probably still get to treat a lot of my favorite cases: equine colic. You could say that horses with tummy aches are kinda my thing, and Dr. Shire operated an equine-only clinic, or so I thought. Little did I know that since this clinic also performed abdominal surgeries for horses, I would treat three hundred or more colicky horses that year.

Dr. Shire was a nice man, short, with a wide and jolly smile and a wife who managed his practice. He had a positive attitude and a love for horses so big that it usually spilled over into his spare time. He was always willing to help a young vet, which was nice. I called him. A lot.

I went to work on my first day with a few simple vaccine appointments. Dr. Shire and I rode around together in his big dually truck, a pickup truck with dual rear tires. Dr. Shire provided me a personal vet vehicle, which was a converted Ford Expedition. I was

114

thrilled. It all seemed so first class. I was also happy to have a year of vet practice under my belt, and I was ready for this next chapter.

On my second day, I showed up to work polished, ready, and Dr. Shire went over my schedule with me. He said, "And I see you are going out to Enterprise Farms call me if you need me." It was like two separate sentences smashed into one as he said them, and it made me think there was something he wasn't saying.

"Anything I should know?" I wondered aloud.

"Well, they don't actually, uh, have horses. Maybe just one or two, but I'm not sure right now."

"Well, what do they have?"

Now I am not a horse novice. I can walk the horse walk and talk the horse talk. Twenty years as an English rider and many years around walking horse people, rodeo folk, pony club people, 4-H clubbers, carriage horses, and the like have made me very comfortable around horses and horse people. I know I am competent to handle most equine cases that's presented, but I am terrified to work on anything with four stomachs (cows, etc.), unless maybe it's a goat, and even then I pull out all my books. Suddenly, I wasn't sure I would just be treating horses. This ruminant-flavored uncertainty crept in and threatened to devour me in front of my new boss.

Dr. Shire explained that Enterprise Farms was a nice place with lots of barns and white fences, and he assured me that there was a large staff for the animals. Then he dropped the bomb: Enterprise Farms was actually a really substantial collection of large exotic animals. I felt the impact in my gut, and in that moment, it was as if I were the one with four stomachs, and every one of them dropped.

"Oh." I tried not to panic. I wanted show Dr. Shire I was ready and competent. I tried to calmly gather more information.

"Is it a petting farm?"

"No," he said. Not adding anything.

"Is it a zoo?"

"Uh, no."

Where was I going?

"So they just have like…a lot of exotic animals on a large piece of land for no reason?"

"Yes. That's it."

"Do they breed the animals maybe?"

"Eh, no."

I could tell he saw my thought process, but he didn't know how to explain a collection of zoo animals with no purpose other than to romp in a field for the entertainment of the owners. To Dr. Shire, they were simply a paying client, and he didn't ask judgmental questions.

"Well, okay." I smiled. "What is the call for, exactly?" *An exotic but small goat maybe.*

"Well, to check a wound." Dr. Shire paused. It was only for a millisecond, but it was long enough for me to know that something was coming. Something strange was coming. "On a camel," he continued. "You'll be fine."

Oh dear. Dang…tartar sauce…bullocks.

"A camel?" I tried to politely ask.

Maybe it's a small camel, I was thinking. *Let it be a small camel.*

Dr. Shire assured me that it would not be so bad, reminding me that there were a lot of good handlers out at Enterprise Farms.

Okay, sure. Not too bad. A wound. I could deal with that. *Maybe.* This back-and-forth played out in my head for a while with half of me feeling ill prepared for the day's assignment and the other half of me acting as a loud, confident life coach, bullying myself into believing I could get through this.

As soon as I got in the truck and drove out of sight, I frantically called Dr. Paca, my beloved vet school professor, to coach me on some camel know-how. Thankfully, I got him on the phone, and he gave me a few tips, mainly involving sedation of Camelids. I was to use a Xylazine-Ketamine-Butorphanol mixture, if I needed it, and he told me the dose and the mixture instructions. He told me there was nothing else he could think of, just sew them up like normal. "And don't get spit on," he chortled into the phone. Then he congratulated me on my new job.

I arrived to a beautiful farm, well hidden from the public. It had a long straight driveway with white fences on both sides as I pulled down the smooth asphalt lane. Expansive pastures with several

116

different types of exotic large animals were on each side of the driveway. Along the road were also rows of perfectly aligned trees, and at the end of the mile-long driveway was a massive plantation home. I drove past zebras, alpacas, gazelles, and oryxes (African antelopes). I pulled into the barn area, and a gruff man in his sixties greeted me. I introduced myself and complimented him on his farm. He said his name was Bob and grumbled that he was not the owner. "Oh," I said. "You're the barn manager then?" I smiled big, trying to be pleasant, wanting to be accepted at every establishment, including this one, as a polite professional.

"No, not a manager or owner or anything with a title." He seemed irritated and just looked at me. *Okay, awkward. Obviously not that happy of a worker. Was my whole day going to be this uncomfortable?* He said the owners lived in the big house and that he never saw them. "I just care for the animals." So, I had met the lead handler for the day, I guess. I told myself it was going to be okay. I didn't quite believe it though.

"So I hear you have a camel with a wound?"

"Oh yes, Filmore. He's over there. Hope you're ready." He chuckled in an unfriendly tone.

Not comforting.

Bob got on the walkie-talkie to call in the recruits; they had to get Filmore. He snickered over the radio to his fellow workers. I fidgeted in my britches. We strolled across the barnyard and across the driveway to a flat, green pasture with four camels. I had not seen them initially when I drove in because they were back by a tree; plus, I was probably so distracted by everything. Three of the camels were large, much larger than horses. Then there was the one in the back corner. Camel number four was completely and utterly enormous.

Deep breaths. It's going to be fine.

Seven or eight men showed up as we approached the fence. The fence itself was curious. It was only two boards high with a white post every five feet or so. It was short as fences go, and there was no electrical wire. "I guess camels don't jump," I thought. I really had no idea.

"Which one is Filmore?"

"He's that big guy."

Of course he is.

"Wow. Umm, just so I know for sure, for dosages and things, how much does he weigh?"

"Oh, about 2,200 pounds."

It had to be the big giant camel who weighs 2,200 pounds. That's two 2s and two 0s, in case you missed it.

"What's wrong exactly?"

"He has a wound on his shoulder. We'll get him for you."

Dang...bullocks...tartar sauce...need to focus. I can do this.

The men decided to feed the camels some grain first. The massive, slow-moving animals strolled to the fence. They happily accepted some grain in their buckets and began to nonchalantly eat. The buckets were evenly spaced hanging on the posts of the pasture. Then someone clipped Filmore's halter, and he instantly objected, backing up some. Then another person clipped his halter on the other side; by now, he was cackling camel profanity at them. Clearly, he wasn't used to this. The foam erupted from between his lips, like he was getting ready to nail someone. Anyone.

Well, this is just great. Then in a moment that was a great blessing amongst the onslaught of stressors, I noticed the wound on his shoulder. It was about four by five centimeters wide. A giant scrape, but nothing that would require stitches. What a relief; so uncomplicated—oh joy, I have found. I climbed up on the fence next to Filmore's massive shoulder to take a closer look. That's when I became horribly aware that the fence was partially rotten, swaying beneath me, and splitting some.

Trying to focus on the wound while rocking back and forth on the shaky fence was no small feat. Suddenly, the workers became scared for me. They yelled at one another in anxiety-filled Spanish. I guess they collectively made a decision to aid me because they placed a large five-gallon bucket on Filmore's head. Alarmed at this, I thought, *Is this really happening? Is this how camel people do it? Is there such a thing as camel people? Maybe in the desert. They certainly did not cover this in my Alabama vet school.* Filmore's camel profanity became more intense. *Why is there a bucket...on his head?*

The bucket was ridiculous, and I knew it. I could not ignore the fact that the 2,200-pound, agitated animal could whack me with his bucket head in a moment, and then probably the fence would give out, and in a perfect trifecta of events, Filmore, bucket-blinded camel, would stomp over my body, making it flush with the dirt and gravel. I foresaw all these events happening.

Common sense, come back to me. I got down.

I asked the handlers to take the bucket off. All the men were shouting, and I silently feared for my life. I prayed. The many handlers said they were trying to keep him from spitting on me. I urgently told them saliva does not bother me. After all, spit is non-toxic and much less traumatic than being pummeled by a giant head with a bucket on it. My assessment of Filmore was that he was not difficult or ferocious. He seemed like possibly a kind soul, but he was miserable by the way he was being handled. I glared at the handlers. They conceded and removed the bucket.

All animals have a threshold. Sometimes, as veterinarians, we see the signs like a cat swatting his tail or a dog jerking his head around fast. There are signs that you are near it. The threshold. We often have to become masterful in both reading the signs, tiptoeing around them, and still trying to get the necessary objective performed, like giving a shot or, in this case, cleaning a wound. Some animals have a low threshold and are set off easily. Others have a high threshold and can tolerate a lot. Sometimes, we pass the threshold. We don't mean to, but then everything in the delicate relationship becomes ten times harder. The animal is now provoked and ready to attack you.

Filmore had a threshold, and I was pretty sure without ever having been around camels before that we were near the breaking point. Once the bucket was removed, though, he eased up just a little. His eyes seemed grateful there was no more bucket. Encouraging, but I was still silently wondering if my participation in this wound care called my sanity into question.

Still questioning my judgment, I tried to climb the fence again. This time, armed with more wound scrubbing materials, I got to the second post and leaned toward the large camel. He was still foaming his saliva all along his lip edges and swishing the froth back and forth like a washing machine. The cackling camel obscenities had eased into mellower bellowing, like soft camel moans. The fence posts, barely in the ground, began to sway. I tried to hang on; Filmore, thankfully, seemed unbothered by me at his shoulder. I leaned toward the wound, scrubbing and applying cream. The fence was tolerating me. Almost there. Seriously, *who does this?*

Almost done, then my camel relations will hopefully cease, and I can go back to the land of horses.

Then Mr. Bob, ground leader with no management title, said, "Oh, and he has diarrhea." Sure enough, the moment he said it, Filmore spurted a liquid brown slush from his rear.

Great, just when I thought I was out of the woods, camel GI medicine, and what do I know about this? Zero. Bob nonchalantly added, "Actually, all them camels have the runs." *Wonderful.*

Not knowing what else to do, I took a sample for a fecal test to check for intestinal parasites. Later in the clinic, I would be thrilled with this split-second decision because it revealed many worm eggs. Bingo.

Once I had the sample, I was excited to be finishing up and to have the enormity of the wound-care saga done. I packed up my things and headed for the vet vehicle. I am sure I looked a bit exasperated, like a girl who had been on a long wagon train expedition. I was weary and dirty, with disheveled hair. I walked with Bob, who carried some of my supplies back to the vet truck. I think he took pity on me. Maybe he was aware of the lack of safety in my camel interaction or he just saw how flustered I was, but he attempted small talk.

"So, how long you been working for Dr. Shire?"

I paused, wondering if I should give an exact, quick answer or avoid the "I'm the super new doc on the job" embarrassment with a long response listing all of my résumé. My mind and energy levels just weren't up for informative, extended responses. I tried to formulate it in my head, but I could not. Just wanting to move on to the next call, I offered just the plain, awkward truth.

"It's my second day," I said. I glanced at Bob and shrugged my shoulders, silently thanking God for safekeeping. Bob raised his eyebrows but said nothing.

Later at the clinic lab, when I realized Filmore and his pasture friends had parasites, I proudly told Dr. Shire of my findings in camel diagnostic medicine, and he seemed pleased by my ability to untangle the diarrhea problem in the camels. He informed me that I would return to Enterprise Farms the following day and give them all shots of Ivermectin, a thick parasiticide medicine that must be injected into the skin of the neck. All four in their four large necks.

Dr. Shire was walking out to go to a call, but he glanced back at me, and added reflectively, "Yep. I think my first patient out there was an elephant."

Alpaca Wars

e go out to Enterprise Farms to give Filmore and his friends
their gigantic doses of Ivermectin to rid them of parasites.
Their skin was tough, about one inch thick. The bucket came
out, the fence swayed, none of the camels were glad about it. I feared
for my life. Who does this? Repeatedly?

The vet clinic office staff member had mentioned in the morning before I left that vaccinations were due for Enterprise Farms' herd
of alpacas. She indicated she had spoken to someone at the farm
about it. I said sure, I could handle that. Dr. Shire had reviewed with
me what vaccines to give, and I had filled the vet truck fridge with
what the animals needed.

When I got to the farm, I mentioned the alpacas' vaccines, but
the handlers seemed dismayed. Apparently, whoever oversaw putting
the alpacas in a small pen that morning had failed to do so. I wanted
to help them if I could—be flexible, wanting to gain approval, that
sort of thing. I said, "Well, can you corral them while I am here?
Does it take long?"

"Well", said Bob the main guy, who was not a manager or
owner or anything, stared at me and my novice unknowingness and
said, "Yeah, I guess we could try." He scratched his head, distressed a
bit. I think my enthusiasm had swayed him into a task he knew was
not so simple.

What came next left me speechless, being a non-Camelid
person.

I pulled the truck around to the area that had the big alpaca
field, and the entire army of handlers was trying to herd them peacefully through a fence and into a small corral. But these creatures were
not passive horses or silent, peaceful, plodding cattle. The alpacas
GREATLY objected. They were armed with militant spitting capabili-

ties, and they fired, repeatedly, copious salivary fluid on the handlers. The handlers tried to band together and continue their mission. They tried various forms of shields to prevent the onslaught of saliva. The alpacas were making horrific sounds from the bottoms of their bellies. They were upset; they were opposed to having their pasture life disturbed. It was like they were screaming: **Why? Why?**

I, being the lady professional, was asked to take refuge. I had a coworker/assistant with me, Dana. She was five feet tall even, had long red hair, and, like me, a longtime horse girl. We hid behind a nearby giant round bale and just peaked around to witness, while the manly men humanely trudged on. I was not opposed to where they had positioned me, nor was Dana.

For twenty minutes or more—what seemed like forever—the workers and the alpacas went on with the whistling, hand waving, shielding, and loogie slinging. The alpacas were now blasting out rank, green spit from the bottoms of their rumens.

Ugh, horrible.

I feel like a terrible person because silently, I started pulling for the alpacas. The men were working so hard, but I began to hope they would become defeated in this task. I'm horrible, I know, but I prefer the horse whisperer approach to large animals as opposed to the rough-and-tumble rodeo. So here is my obvious dilemma: a confession, a deep, building desire from deep inside me. Truth, **I did not want to poke the alpacas**.

Clearly, they were not going to be happy with that.

The men, covered in green loogies, now had ten of the thirty alpacas in the small corral. Oh dear, the men were making a comeback. Should I speak now?

These highly rattled, aggressive, rabid-looking creatures were past any behaviorist threshold, if they ever had one. I knew vaccinating would be most unpleasant, but I just kept quiet behind my giant hay bale. I was desperately trying to override my wimpyness. Dana stared at me, wide-eyed; she didn't say it, but I knew she too was secretly wishing that this would not pan out. We turned and peeked out at the scene.

Finally, after a moderate lull, Bob approached me. The saliva from the alpacas had soaked his hair, his shirt, his jeans, and his face. In addition, it stunk. Poor Bob, he actually wasn't such a bad guy. He swiped a giant loogie-colored saliva slug from his eyelid and slung it to the ground.

UGH! Yuck.

He appeared weary. He said maybe it would be better if we waited until next time the clinic must come out so the staff will be better prepared.

"Okay, sure, no problem," I said.

Lost with the Dirty Bomber

Still year two, I was practicing at Dr. Shire's equine hospital. That year, 2001 or perhaps 2002, we received a lot of sick-horse referrals at our establishment. I was on call every third weekend. Routinely, I came in for the condition called colic. This is a common condition in horses where the intestines get irritated, obstructed, impacted, or twisted. It requires a vet to come out, evaluate the horse, and assess if the horse has a medical colic or a surgical colic. Medical colic is usually treated with pain medication, like Banamine. Mineral oil via a stomach tube usually is also given as a treatment. Surgical colic is much more expensive and requires a hospital with anesthesia equipment for horses and a recovery stall that has thickly matted sides for them to wake up in.

Our equine hospital had all these things. We would often get cases in from all over for us to assess whether the horse had medical or surgical colic. The clinic had twenty to thirty stalls that often were occupied. There were equine vet nurses who would monitor them during the day and administer treatments as prescribed while the vets were out during the day on the farm calls.

One day, I came in late from farm calls, and everyone was gone. I walked by a patient that we'd had for several days and noticed he was quiet in his stall and his head was a bit low. This horse had an indwelling stomach tube, because he had a condition called anterior enteritis. The stomach tube was a direct tube from the side of a nostril and down into the stomach. In this disease, the horses produce a large amount of gastric fluid that they cannot vomit, because horses cannot vomit. The massive distension of the stomach makes them horribly uncomfortable. This condition usually presents the horse as very sick. When you stick a gastric tube in the horse, you see a tremendous amount of dark fluid appear in your bucket from the stomach. This is a very good indication of anterior enteritis, but there are other possibilities. This horse was recovering from his ordeal, but we regularly would help him out by emptying the buildup of "reflux" in his stomach via the indwelling gastric tube. To keep the horse from having to repeatedly be tubed via his nose and esophagus, we just left the tube in place and tied it to the halter with a syringe plunger for a plug. We would use this setup to evacuate the stomach fluids a few times a day, especially for a horse in this condition.

I decided to look at him before I left to go home. I was on call that night. I called my boss, as it was his case, to tell him what the horse's vital signs were and ask if he wanted me to do anything else. The horse seemed stable, or maybe he was just sleeping. "See if he will eat some grass," Dr. Shire said. This is often an indicator that the horse is better. If he bends his neck down and eagerly goes for some green grass, that's always a happy sight for a recovering colic.

So, I did, except I didn't notice the stomach tube wasn't plugged.

I took the horse outside, and he was thrilled. He happily lunged for the grass.

That's when the shower began, a shower of stomach liquids, raining over me. His eager bending had contracted his stomach muscles, which increased pressure in his abdomen, and this, in turn, caused a fountain of gastric fluid right out of his stomach tube into the air and all over me.

It was on my clothes, on my arms, and in my hair. I was instantly repulsed. It dripped down my face. I finished caring for the horse and put him back in the stall and ran into the office. There was a bathroom, but no shower; and as hard as I looked before I left, there was no change of clothes. *Long sigh.* **Great.**

I looked in the mirror. All I had was some paper towels to wipe the stuff off my skin. The smell was appalling. It was on all of me. I am a horse girl, but I am also a bit of a girly girl. I can usually hang with horsey smells, but this is not what I was planning for.

My husband had been gone for months on deployment and was finally back. He was at home, waiting for me to get there. We were newlyweds still, and I was less than thrilled that I had to go home this way.

At this time, I lived on a military base. Since 9/11, the base had become very strict about who gets on base and who gets off. It was especially particular about vehicle paperwork. For a long time, I could get three-month passes for my vet truck, and they would let me through. They did not like it that I was not the owner of the truck. This base had many types of weapons, power plants, ships, and a brig (military prison). Who got on base was a very big deal.

So, it was this night as I was driving home that I realized my gate pass was expired. I groaned.

I stepped out of my truck and walked into the military car pass office. I was cleaned up some, but in desperate need of a shower. Let's not forget that I like looking pristine and this was an utter atrocity, just based on smell alone.

And of course, as luck would have it, I stepped in the door and found a line. A long line. At least ten people in front of me, a small office, and I had horse-stomach contents in my hair. Just in case anyone is doubting at this point, yes, this is a true story. Each person had to slowly explain to the attendant why his or her pass was expired and why a new one was needed. She seemed like a grumpy character. One by one, with obvious disapproval, she slowly addressed the individual cases. I glanced and scanned to find somewhere to hide or step away to spare my fellow line-standers from the reflux fumes, but alas, there was nothing.

Now, I said that the military base never cared for my scenario much. As a vet on call, in a vet truck I didn't own, they were always irritated at me. This night, they decided that they were going to make all folks of business-owned vehicles (just me) go to the back gate and be searched. Uh, okay, wherever that was.

I sighed. I just wanted to get home.

Thankfully, no calls came in during what followed next.

Just to help you imagine, I lived in a very Southern state. There were a lot of marshes everywhere that I often miss, because I found them beautiful. They do, in this part of the country, harbor some fantastic bugs. I have never had allergies in my entire life, but these bugs are so diverse. There was one that my body was and is very opposed, these little black flies. If they bite me, I end up with big purple welts.

I drove four miles to the back gate and drove the truck in. The officer and his colleagues, who seemed nice, searched the vehicle. I got out and stood while the guys went through medications, the endoscope, the dewormers…the castration devices.

"Um, please don't play with that."

"Yes, ma'am."

I finally got back in the vet truck. It was about 9:00 p.m. at this point, and dark. I had been on the phone with my husband, venting all my extremely weary, smelly frustrations. He had calmly listened. (Years later, he would admit that he had chuckled profusely after hanging up the phone.)

I was sitting on the seat, and I realized I had never tried to get to my home from this gate. I rolled down the window. The nice officer, who seemed to cringe, probably at the smell, told me how to get where I needed to be. It was so utterly confusing. I didn't write it down. I was too mad and flustered to bother, which, of course, was not a good decision.

I roughly remember it like this:

Go straight then veer left, then go right at the second street, then take the first right then the first left, then go over a bridge then go left again and after a mile, go right.

While he spoke, I just stared blankly.

"Okay, thanks." My brain was way full of frustration for all that. I drove off. *I'll just figure it out.*

I rolled up the window. It must have been my "perfume," because a swarm of gnats decided to join me in my vet truck. Wonderful. As soon as I was able, I called my husband to vent some more.

He told me he loved me.

He told me to remain calm.

I was not calm, and in about five minutes, I was lost. I saw military facilities, what looked like a nuclear power plant, then missiles. I turned again and again, and with every turn, my panic grew.

I called my husband and told him to call the base police; I was lost. I just knew they were going to see some random white vehicle circling around and charge at me. He said he would not call the base police, that I would figure it out. Then he added, he believed in me. *What? I hung up.*

I was now a girl enraged.

It did not help my situation.

That's when I turned and pulled into…a brig. For those of you who are unaware, that's a military prison. Big barbed-wire fences and brick building. Oh my gosh. I am a little suburban girl, and I was terrified.

I started to itch. But confusion and now panic were distracting me.

The itchiness became worse. I called again, "Marshall, I AM LOST. I can see the BRIG, and the BUGS are BITING ME. The military men are going to start shooting at me!"

I could almost hear the concealed snort coming from the other end of the line.

Outrage.

"I am lost with the dirty bomber!" (He was incarcerated at the prison I had stumbled upon, I knew that much.)

"June, you are going to be okay." I could hear him comfortably sautéing dinner in the background.

The bugs were biting me all over; I have no doubt that they were big fans of my new hair product.

I scratched at my scalp and waved frantically in the front window to try to get them out. I circled the truck and circled until finally, I saw the entrance gate again. I went back to the guard.

He looked shocked to see me. It had been twenty minutes or more.

I said calmly, like a controlled woman withholding fury, "Sir, could you please give me the directions again?"

"Oh yes, ma'am."

I listened better this time, trying to contain my sanity. I made it over the bridge this time, and I knew where I was.

The itchiness had become horrible. I was clawing at my sides and my shoulders and my hair. I stopped at a stop sign and turned on the indoor light to the truck. I was covered in purple splotches. They were all over me, like wallpaper. My long hair was crispy like hair-sprayed hair, only it was not hair spray that had dried in my hair. *Gross.*

I ran into my house, yelling, crying, venting, pouring all my pent-up frustrations out, all while running for the shower. Marshall, after a long stare of disbelief in the spotted spectacle of me, began to laugh. It was such a site to behold. I stared at him with my look of outrage. *So great*, he cried, chuckling with utter joy.

I scowled without words, eyes harsh.

He coughed and quickly went and got me some Benadryl.

God granted me some great mercy—I had no calls that night.

Involving a 911 Operator

My new boss, Dr. Shire, preferred performing a routine equine castration surgery in a different way than my previous employer. My first boss would sedate them so they were lying down and out under anesthesia with a drug combination. My second boss talked me into just performing said procedure while the horse was standing. However, this is not a story about surgery; this is a story about a most uncommon veterinary patient, a human.

I was scheduled to work. It was a Friday, as I recall. There was a different group of assistants working that day, including a fellow—we'll call him Will—in vet tech school whom I had not met before, but I had heard everyone mention him often. He was the dependable type, raised on a farm, dedicated to veterinary medicine. We met, and I told him I was signed up to go do a castration on a six-month-old Arabian and asked if he would come and hold the horse while I was performing the surgery. I told him I was going to perform the surgery with the horse standing, a new approach for me. He agreed, and off we went to the case together.

We arrived at the stable, privately owned as I recall. We were greeted by an older man with a thick eastern European accent. He seemed friendly. We followed him around back to his stable. He showed us where the young colt was. My assistant went to the colt's head while I gave the injection, and I performed the local anesthesia as well. The colt became super sleepy. My assistant held his head and used a common tool on the tip of his nose called a rope twitch, just in case. A twitch tends to put a horse in a mild trance. Everything was in place; horse was sedated. Local anesthesia effective. Trained helper at horse's head. Should be smooth sailing, right?

I got through the first part of the surgery, nervous, but it went well. Just to clarify, remember, my head is next to this colt's hind legs, and I am underneath his belly to do the surgery this way. I had one testicle removed and one to go. I remember looking up out of the corner of my eye, just to make sure that all was well at the head of the horse, and I saw Will's eyes droop, and then his whole body slumped down like a sack of potatoes onto the floor, completely unconscious.

I jumped up (carefully) and ran over to Will. I yelled his name several times; the owner came over, concerned as well and started yelling at my assistant and slapping his face.

I frantically got him to stop slapping my guy. "Ah, man, he's out!" said my European owner. I told him to go call 911. He ran off to his house to do this. The colt just stood there in his sedated slumber, obliviously clinging to uniball status.

I stared down at this poor fellow who appeared to be out cold. I told myself I was a doctor, new maybe, and not for humans for sure, but I had *some* knowledge, and I should do **something**. I took out my stethoscope and listened to Will's heart. He had a good heartbeat. That's good. I looked at his chest; he was breathing, slowly and steadily. I took a pulse at his wrist, I knew that much. It was good.

Well, what else should I check? CRT, aka capillary refill time? That's an indicator of shock if it's slow or if perfusion is slow. But I did not know at that time how to check this in a human; I only knew how to do it for other mammals. So, deciding I had nothing to lose, I lifted poor Will's lip and looked at his gum color. Pink, that's good. Then, with my big thumb, I pressed on his gums. Yes, I did. Happy to report that it was normal. (Later, a nurse would kindly inform me that they only press on fingernails to get that measurement, but my way was adequate.)

So, it gets crazier.

Back comes the owner. He has a portable phone in his hand and is yelling at the 911 operator, but the conversation is so wrong. He is screaming, "We were gelding a horse! Ya know what that means. Gelding, like castrating it. It's when you take the testicles…" He began explaining the equine procedure in greater detail to this poor, probably nonhorsey person. From fifteen feet away, I could hear the frustration in the voice of the 911 operator coming through the phone. She screamed, "Just tell me about the human! What's wrong with the PERSON?" At that, the owner handed the phone to me. I said to her, "My assistant seems to be out cold. I think he might have fainted, but I'm not sure."

Right as I was beginning to tell her about what I saw, Will woke up. He looked like he felt yucky. We were all staring. I explained what happened to him. I asked if he thought he could have fainted, and he nodded. We spoke with him and went back and forth with the 911 operator, who seemed much more collected and calm, for a while. Will said he had not had much for breakfast. I thanked the operator after she felt that Will was okay, and we got off the phone.

After several minutes, Will told me repeatedly that he was fine and he wanted to get back to work. My colorful owner got him a bucket, which Will sat on and held the lead. My colt was still happily enjoying his drugs, and he had his second testicle removed without interruption. Yeah!

As we made our way back to the truck, I tried to make my dedicated assistant feel better, consoling, empathizing, etc. He looked a bit down about what had happened. He was a student, after all. I said it happens sometimes to lots of folks in medicine. I told Will that it had happened to me before, too, but far worse, because afterward, I got really sick and threw up. To which he stared blankly at me for a long moment and then ran off in the woods to empty his own poor nauseous stomach. I stood sadly and watched. The owner came and stood next to me and watched for a while, shaking his head.

Later, Will informed me he had been medically checked out, was fine, and was into eating good breakfasts.

Kitty rubbed her forehead and ran her fingers through her hair, *What do I do with this call?*

Ms. Curl decided to turn the conversation to the original point of calling the clinic. It was not related to her alien-infested house.

She said, "My cat, Princess Fluff, has recently become very ill, losing weight, and vomiting. I am so scared because the vomit contains the alien's babies. The babies look like the adult aliens, just smaller."

Kitty had nothing to offer at this point.

She became deeply concerned for whatever ailment the feline— and the human—may have.

Ms. Curl continued on. She had figured out the life cycle. "The aliens have taken over my Persian cat's body and that is how they reproduce, inside of the cat, and then she vomits up the babies." Her frantic voice hurried on, "It's so horrible! I'm just worried about my cat, poor Princess Fluff! She's going to die of alien infestation if no one helps her!"

"Calm down, Ms. Curl, it's gonna be okay. Are you okay?"

No answer.

"Can you bring her in? Princess Fluff? Today? Or as soon as possible?"

"Yes, I will be right there, and I am bringing one of the alien babies she threw up. It's in a plastic baggie."

"Okay, be careful."

"Oh, I will. I can handle 'em"

"Are you coming now? Yes, and you will have the alien?" Kitty bewildered.

Ms. Curl responded, "Yes, it's not hard to get you a sample, they are everywhere!"

The Happy Couple Picks Out a Puppy

My loving husband I had been married for three years when we realized we needed a second dog. We had just had a baby and moved north, and my parents had graciously brought my long-time best buddy, Camp, to join us in our newly purchased home. It was cold in the new area, and Camp had been on a farm. He had been happy to see me, and we still ran together, but he seemed depressed. I figured he must've liked all the horses and acres at my parents' house. Now he was in Cleveland, Ohio. It's cold there; it snows six months a year, and I had no other pets, just a six-month-old baby boy.

We had talked about what kind of dog to get. My husband was specific about what he wanted. He first said he wanted an English bulldog; I said no, too many health problems. We were combing through the paper, looking at the ads, when he stumbled across one for basset hounds. "That's what I want," he said. A basset! "They're okay, right?""

Uh, yeah, I guess.

In vet school, I used to take care of two basset hounds at Ms. Wendy's house, my good friend and mentor, to earn money. She had many animals including the horses and, of course, the guinea fowl. The bassets were well-adored pets. I have many a fond memory of their slow easy tail-wagging greetings.

We decided to answer an ad for a mommy basset who was for sale at a low price. A side point, I will never again buy a dog. My family had always found dogs, adopted them, and named them after the location you found them. Stewart was found at Stewarts Grocery store. Camp was found at a kids' camp where I taught riding. But now, I was going to a breeder and looking at her mommy dog.

There is often, but not always, a tense relationship that exists between breeders and veterinarians. Breeders will dish out information on what is best for their breed and frequently, in my experience, tell owners to ignore what veterinarians say. Owners will sometimes only listen to this often-misguided information from a breeder and more often than not end up with the problems that their educated, student-loan-burdened veterinarian was trying to avoid. I have had this experience time after time, unfortunately. It can be highly frustrating.

So there, that's it; often, it's a difficult relationship. I will say, "It's not all breeders that work this way." Thank you to all the clients and the breeders out there who respect the opinion of the veterinarian over Dr. Google or otherwise. We worked hard to be a knowledgeable professional for you.

However, this would affect me in my personal life.

We go out to look at this basset. Her name is Darcy. I figure she is great because she was discounted for being older, she was sweet, and in a home with kids, and she was POTTY-TRAINED. I, of course, could spay her. I did not need to deal with that whole puppy bit and a new baby AND a husband who was about to deploy.

I was humoring my husband by allowing him to pick out this dog and let it be "his." Camp was my dog; he was a therapy dog, and he had been a close companion of mine through vet school. Camp was our dog, but really he was my dog.

We drove out in the snow, and my baby fell asleep in the backseat. Marshall was super excited. I said, "Well, you can go in first. Don't tell the breeder I'm a vet!"

"Okay," he said and jumped out. I stopped him once more.

"What?" he said.

"This dog just had some puppies, I think they are like four weeks old or something. So just remember: we're just here to look at the momma dog."

"Uh, okay."

What a mistake that was.

I am sitting in the car watching my husband introduce himself. There is snow all around—it was October in Cleveland, after all. Snow does not leave Cleveland usually until the following April or May (and locals will joke about seeing it in June).

He comes out of the house minutes later with something in his hand and an eager, flushed look. Much to my dismay, he is carrying a tiny little basset puppy in one hand. He looks totally bewildered and enamored. (*Oh no!*) He knocks on the car window. I didn't want to roll it down, I knew where this was going, but he eagerly knocked some more. I obliged.

"Honey! Look at this! Have you ever seen anything so cute?!"

This puppy was very cute; however, I know puppies and see them often. Her giant ears were as long as her tiny little body. It's a rare human who wouldn't have gotten all mushy at the sight of her.

"Um, yes, dear, it's a nice puppy. Please put it back. We are here to look at the mom, 'kay? The adult...*the potty-trained one.*"

"Well, why can't we just get a puppy?"

Let's just revisit the fact that this is a full-grown military man.

"Let's just go see the momma dog."

"Aw, I want the puppy!"

He looked completely disappointed and defeated. He shrugged his shoulders and held the little puppy close to his chest.

I woke up my baby boy and put him on my hip. I went to meet this breeder who had lured my susceptible husband into her puppy trap. The puppies were twice as much money as the momma dog. *Grrrrrr.*

We walked together to the door. I requested that the crafty breeder show me the momma dog. My husband said nothing. She brought Darcy out. Darcy was sweet. I really liked her. She had a slow steady wag to her tail and calm mannerisms. My husband looked at her with his nose stiff up in the air, still clinging to his puppy.

I said to him, "She looks great, we should get her. She and Camp would be great friends." My husband, still biased completely, said, "No, a puppy would be better."

The breeder agreed with him, of course (puppy = more money).

I looked at my husband with frustration and disapproval. "I don't want a puppy, I don't want to have to potty-train in the winter, with a baby, and you're about to be deployed!"

The breeder chimed in, "You know it only takes two weeks to potty-train a puppy."

This was outrageous. I was still <u>not</u> going to tell her that I was in the know.

"No, I'm not buyin' that," I said defiantly, definitely out of character for me.

My husband desperately sided with the breeder. "Honey, she says two weeks, she knows, just two weeks. She's a *breeder*!"

Oh my gosh, this is ridiculous.

Just ignore your wife. WHAT *does she know*? (A lot about it, actually!)

We eventually excused ourselves to go have a marital discussion by the car. The puppy was still in the crook of my husband's arm.

We tried to talk about it. My husband—MY HUSBAND—still was convinced that just because the breeder said it was so, it was so. Six weeks old, and she can be house trained in two weeks. **Whatever.** I would later learn that this breed also has a stubborn side of epic proportions. Trainers would turn us away because she was a basset hound.

That's when he said it. And it just got me, so got me. Full-grown man, sad voice...

"I've never had my own puppy."

He cuddled the three-pound pup next to his face and neck, like something that was missing from his childhood.

Sigh. Unbelievable. Really?

"Okay," I said. "I give up. Give her the money. We'll come back when she's fully weaned and I'll have a stethoscope with me!"

We named her Baggywrinkle, a sailing term. It seemed to fit a floppy-skinned, giant-eared puppy. She was highly energetic, full of mischief, and often tripped on her own ears. She played with Camp some but often just ran him out of his own bed. My husband cuddled with her for two weeks then got deployed, of course. She did end up being really great with my kids, toddler years included, and their friends. Despite following all current recommendations for house training, her housebreaking took months and months—and then a few more months. Well, at least I am correct about some things.

Stormy Southern Nights

I would now like to introduce Dr. Tammy Calico, my good friend. Dr. Tammy Calico was working deep in the South. She is a mild-mannered, kind person with a petite frame and a large scale of compassion. She is always reserved, highly knowledgeable, and soft-spoken. She had been in practice for two years in an equine and small-animal clinic at the time of this craziness. Her practice, since it treats horses, usually involves having to drive to where the horses are.

Dr. Calico had just gotten off from work and was eating her dinner when she received a call from a hyped-up man that his horse had a stick through his head. She tried to calm the caller some, but ultimately, she promised she was on her way. She took down the address, called her boss to confirm that he was a client, and headed out. It was an address she had never been to, north side of town by the fairgrounds. She looked outside and noticed a massive storm was coming, and the wind had picked up. She sighed but, being super concerned for the poor horse in pain with a branch in his head, she got in her truck and left.

She went to the address but circled around some trailer parks multiple times in the vet truck. This was a few years before the luxuries of GPS. The storm began to rage with rain and wind. She saw a horse pasture with horses, not the exact address, but decided to go ahead and knock on the trailer door anyway.

"Hello, sir, did you call for a vet?"

A large man with a Harley Davidson bandana answered the door. He was dressed from head to toe in leather motorcycle gear.

"No, I have no idea what you are talking about. My horses are fine," he gruffly stated.

"Okay, well, can you please help me? Do you know where this address is, or where Scott Smith lives?"

"No, I have no idea," he said, then inappropriately shut the door. In her face.

As Dr. Calico was leaving, she noticed a long drive with the correct address. It led to a mansion. It seemed close to what her directions had stated. However, she saw no horses and no barn. She was supposed to go to the barn. It was now about 9:00 or 10:00 p.m., and rain was whipping at her from all angles.

She decided to go to the mansion and knock on the enormous front doors. No one answered. That's when she heard it—a shushing. She glanced about but saw no one. She rang the doorbell again.

"Shhhhhhhh."

Dr. Calico looked off to the side of the porch, and there was an elderly woman in the front bushes. She seemed to be crouching down inside the bushes. Before she could ask if the woman needed help, the woman looked at her and said "SHHHHHHH!" then anxiously whispered, "He doesn't like visitors."

"Who? Are you okay? What are you talking about?" Dr. Calico, extremely frightened, stepped toward the woman in the bushes.

"He doesn't like visitors! You should leave! Go, go now!"

Dr. Calico started to quickly step down from the porch when a man came charging out from the back side of the house with purpose and anger. Also, he was in a wheelchair. He had a shotgun in his lap. Yes, this really happened to poor sweet Dr. Calico, one of the most nonthreatening vets I have ever met.

He appeared to be incredibly thin and feeble, a mere skeleton with skin, shrunken into his wheelchair in every way. He was yelling a multitude of obscenities, and every part of him was in a ferocious rage. Despite obvious frailty, he operated the wheelchair like a pro contender. He chased, with relentless zeal, poor Dr. Calico to her truck.

In sheer panic, Dr. Calico jumped in her massive vet truck, fired it up, and backed out, fearing for her life. She backed right over his entire flower garden, squealed her tires in the nice mulch, and took out an entire line of decorative post and rail fencing. She did not care. She needed to leave, now.

Because she is the incredibly compassionate person that I described, somehow, concern for the horse still dictated her next action. As she was pulling away from a feeble man in a wheelchair with a shotgun and extreme potty mouth, she found another driveway. It seemed closer to the original description of where she was supposed to go. She had not noticed it before. She turned down and sped down it, hoping it was right.

It led to a barn.

She pulled in, and a superexcited man greeted her. He said his name was Scott. He was so hyped up, he looked like his eyeballs might pop out. He fidgeted continuously while he spoke.

"Okay, finally, I am in the right spot," she thought, *but Mr. Scott is acting odd.*

Great.

Dr. Calico explained that she had accidentally gone to the mansion.

"Oh yeah, that's who I rent the barn from. He doesn't like visitors much," said Mr. Scott.

"I, uh, figured that out." Dr. Calico took a deep breath.

Mr. Scott anxiously told her the drama of his horse and found her in the field. It was absolutely horrible. Stick in the head, horrible, terrible emergency. Mr. Scott went ahead and informed Dr. Calico that he is an extremely experienced horse person, that he runs the best operation, and he sidetracked into telling her that he was actually the best person for horses and horse care that he knew. He found himself to be, well, really great.

"Uh, okay," she said, still uneasy.

The horse was standing quietly on the cross ties. (Cross ties are two lead ropes that come from the sides of the barns and attach to opposite sides of the horse's halter.) Dr. Calico looked up at the horse; he was calm and appeared gentle. He had a large stick in a long black forelock, but there was no blood anywhere. The front mane, the forelock, was horribly tangled.

Dr. Calico gently moved the hair around. The stick had not penetrated the skin at all. It was just stuck in a knot in the forelock. Dr. Calico realized as she was detangling the mane and the stick, that none of this was truly emergency status. All this drama, complete with two hours of driving in a storm, for a hair knot.

She calmly told Mr. Scott that his horse did not need any advanced care or surgery or medicine, that the stick was just caught in the mane.

Mr. Scott seemed dismayed.

Despite it being now about 11:00 p.m., he asked if she would mind doing a physical on his new llama. "Just to make sure it's healthy. I really would like to know," he said. He was serious.

"Um, no, you have to schedule that," a weary Dr. Calico said.

"Well, can you pull some Coggins tests and do vaccines on my other horses while you are here?" (Routine care stuff.)

"Um, no, sir. We will schedule it for daytime."

Flustered, she had raced out to this call, in a storm, gotten lost, eventually gotten chased by a man with a shotgun in a wheelchair, all for a stick caught in the mane of a horse that was owned by a guy who had questionable behavior.

"Well, would you like to come in my trailer and dry off?"

Creepy! Ahhhhhhhhhh.

"No, sir, I just need to go." And with that, having successfully cured the horse with stick coming out of his head, she left and made it home safe.

Dr. Calico got to her house, called her boss, and vented to that guy for forty-five minutes straight.

The clinic received an angry call that next day demanding that it pay for a fence and some flowers.

Personally, I'm just glad my good vet friend was okay!

Rancid

This story is for the many, many vet support staffs I have worked with. Just so you know, you are greatly appreciated. However, stories like this story frustrate the vet staff to no end. But this is my most treasured case of it. It perfectly exemplifies a scenario I know happens a lot in the vet world: a concerned vet worker determined to be a good detective and an owner who can't remember. Often, folks just need a moment.

I was working in the northern part of the country, and we had six veterinarians at our practice. The practice was mixed animal, but I was hired to be primarily small animal and occasionally to chime in on the equine stuff. We had all the latest equipment and a well-trained staff. I grew a lot in my skills in ultrasonography and chemotherapy at this clinic. It was a fun and exciting place to work.

After working there for six or eight months, I was doing well and had gotten used to the staff. There were two highly trained licensed vet technicians who managed a lot of the surgeries and hospitalized cases. The clinic hospital manager decided to hire one more, a nice brunette with a short stature named Jacky Boston. Jacky, although being nice and cordial, appeared to be on the radar of the only other female veterinarian, Dr. Torti, who was also a part clinic owner.

Jacky was also having a tough time fitting in with her coworkers. She was receiving a lot of sass from the other two technicians, Heather and Sara. Jacky had confidence in her abilities, and she had a quiet, serious personality. I personally did not have any trouble with her at all, but I tend to just kind of like everyone I meet, most of the time.

One day during morning appointments, I watched Jacky and Dr. Torti work up a case together. I remember Dr. Torti sending Jacky back in the room four times because she had not asked every single possible question on a case history. Jacky seemed to take it in stride. It seemed like horrible overkill on the new hire, so I asked Dr. Torti about it. She glared at me. Then she explained, "Jacky seems a bit arrogant in my opinion. I am just trying to prove a point." I think Dr. Torti thought Jacky was a bit of a know-it-all, and she didn't like it one bit, nor would she tolerate it.

All righty then. I guess I will stay out of it.

Anyway, most of the time Jacky just worked with me, and she did a great job. She helped me in surgery. She helped me in ultrasound. She helped me with my multiple chemo patients that I had at the time. We joked and fretted over the same things. She treated my many hospitalized cases. She helped with the owners. She did seem to have, although always under wraps, a side of her that could be labeled as temperamental.

But shortly after Dr. Torti had tried to make a point to Jacky, we had a diarrhea case that presented to the clinic. It was terrible. There were two Bassett hounds, and they both had bloody diarrhea and bloody vomitus. They illustrated this all over our waiting area.

The front receptionists panicked from the mess and hustled them in a room. Jacky looked at me. She said, with her bruised confidence, "Don't worry I will ask *all* the questions."

Now, every pet nurse has always taken pride in trying to help the veterinarian solve the mystery. Here were two sick puppies that got sick together. This would tend to suggest that it was something they were exposed to or something they ate.

I have, for many years, noticed the great joy a pet nurse, a pet assistant, or a vet tech experiences if she uncovers the mystery to profound itching with a flea comb. Then the pet nurse is able to show the flea to an owner, who is in what we veterinarians like to call "flea denial." Sometimes, they are excited because in their history-taking, they stumbled across a piece of history that involves giving "people food," like bacon, to the pet twelve hours before. This is part of their job, and they take great pride in being able to do it well and uncover helpful clues for the veterinarian. It is a wonderful and helpful skill to be able to take a good history and recognize what to ask and what is not as pertinent. It helps a doctor be much more efficient.

Jacky was out to prove that she had this skill, the subjective, with the knowledge of a licensed vet tech. She was determined to discover what had ailed these two hounds before I ever saw them. Surely, it was something a good history would reveal. Into the room she went.

She came out of the room thirty minutes later.

She had asked about every toxin, every "people food," any possible dietary changes, any exposure to other dogs, drinking from puddles, any time out for walks, if the pets had been out of town, any new flea products, any new dogs, or changes to the environment. She went 'round and 'round with the people about what could have possibly set off these two dogs. They were up to date on vaccines and preventative care. She collected some samples and took their temperatures. The pets had been getting progressively worse over twenty-four hours. They were young adult dogs, about two years old each. Jacky and I discussed every angle. Yet based on the information she had gathered, there appeared to be no reason whatsoever for the illness. The two pets had no changes and never went out of the yard. This was what these owners told her at the end of her extremely long and thorough history taking.

I went in the room to look and do my part about five or ten minutes later.

I introduced myself and did the normal pleasant exchanges with the owners. I started to examine these two patients. They were mildly dehydrated, and both had fevers. They had mildly painful abdomens. Jacky, after she had set up all her samples, came in to join me and hold for me as I finished the exams. She quietly looked on as I did my job.

I looked up at the owners somewhat perplexed. "Are you sure you don't know what could've set off their tummies?"

"No," said one of the owners. She mindlessly shook her head.

Then she added, "Well, ya know, we did feed them both some RANCID deer meat a few days ago, but that's okay, right? I mean we couldn't eat it, smelled terrible, but they're dogs, right? So, we figured they would be fine, and we gave it to them."

(Note: Owner actually did use the word **rancid**.)

I stared for a moment, about to say that actually *no, that was not okay for dogs, and yes, it was the probable cause.*

Then I saw something out of the corner of my eye, or maybe it was a feeling of something as hot as the sun. I glanced. It was Jacky, and she had a line of red traveling up her face, until it hit the top of her forehead, and now she looked back at me—she was just red/purple, like someone holding their breath. Maybe she was, but one thing was for sure: she was **upset**. I could silently envision the steam of frustration pouring out of her ears. She had tried so hard on this one. *I hid my smirk best I could, but it was really hard.*

Jacky did not say a word. She just stood there, engulfed in red, as I spoke about things that are rotten and harbor bacteria, like food poisoning in humans. I tried not to laugh and to stay professional about why this was not okay. I went into treatment with IV fluids, antibiotics, and hospitalization. The owners agreed to all recommendations. When I got out of the room, I had a good chuckle over it. Jacky just stared at me, speechless, shaking her head, like she wanted to cry. After a few more minutes, she began slowly turning back to a normal color. Jacky had managed to control it. I told her I knew her history taking was totally solid and was totally proud that she kept her cool. That scenario of remembering important things only when the doctor walks in happens a lot.

Some folks just need a minute to sit and think.

Points of this story:

1. It is never okay to feed a pet rotting deer meat, or anything RANCID, really.
2. Often, people need a moment after they've been quizzed on the spot about all possibilities to recall what was out of place in their routines.
3. Pet nurses, vet assistants, vet students, and vet techs get very frustrated by number 2.

Where's My Shoe?

This is Dr. Cassie Corgi's story from her third or fourth year in practice.

Dr. Corgi had moved on from her rural practice to a small-animal practice in the heart of an upscale suburban neighborhood.

She had been working here for a while when she met a nice, very tall, well-dressed woman with a wildly energetic cocker spaniel. The woman was Ms. Brittany. She was middle age, probably in her forties and had Gucci glasses and Coach purses. She always dressed well, kind of like she was the CEO of a company, and she carried herself like it too. Her outfits had one feature that seemed slightly out of place: she wore Croc shoes. Maybe a woman who enjoys foot comfort, whatever—good for you, honey!

Ms. Brittany had a little black cocker named Midnight, who was super hyper all the time and had not one ounce of self-control. Ms. Brittany came to the clinic a lot for common cocker reasons—ears, skin, ears, dietary indiscretion with bowels, more ear problems, and nail trims—and she gave a lot of opinions on Midnight's care and what was to be done and not done.

She always demanded to see Dr. Corgi. Dr. Corgi liked Ms. Brittany but knew she always required extra attention. Her pet was friendly, but sometimes she was so friendly, it could make things challenging.

One day, Ms. Brittany came in for a scheduled recheck appointment. She was quiet and poised, as usual, with her little dog at her feet, shaking its body all over in pure-excitement wiggles. Dr. Corgi and the nurse came in, and Midnight lunged toward them and jumped from one to the other, licking and wiggling. Ms. Brittany wanted Midnight's ears rechecked after two weeks of treatment.

"Midnight, come here," and with that, Midnight ran to Ms. Brittany and jumped at her legs.

Ms. Brittany leaned down and picked up Midnight and set her on the table for the vet assistant, who had to act fast to hang on. This action of being so close to new people sent Midnight into an overjoyed state of mind. The excitement began to pour out of every centimeter of her little body. The assistant was trying to just get her to calm down, but she was receiving an onslaught of endless tongue licks, so much so she could not open her eyes, or her mouth, for that matter. Dr. Corgi joined in. She put her stethoscope on Midnight's chest, which kicked the dog's joyfulness into overdrive. Midnight turned into a small Bronco of excitement jollies. She now had two people wanting to give her attention. Her enthusiasm for this treat beyond all treats was too much.

Licking, wiggling, Midnight was swinging her head enthusiastically between Dr. Corgi and her assistant.

"Okay," said Dr. Corgi. "Now I'm gonna look in your ears, little girl."

Which, of course, was next to impossible, like asking a hummingbird to remain still. Midnight could not be restrained. This seemed to be way more attention than she had ever imagined (even though she came to the vet regularly).

Dr. Corgi tried once to see in the ears and wondered if maybe this pet had eaten some caffeinated dog biscuits. She attempted again—no luck. Vet assistant was still unable to open eyes—poor girl.

With this, Ms. Brittany stood in front of the dog. She quietly reached down and pulled off her shoe. Then almost like flipping a switch, she took on the look of an angry mother. A mother much beyond exasperation and reason.

Ms. Brittany lifted the shoe over the dog's head and yelled, "Midnight! WHERE'S MY SHOE?"

She swung it in the air and swirled it over the dog's head. She had the look of a possessed woman who was not going to take the nonsense anymore. It looked like she was going to give this little pup a massive slap. Her eyes were wide and purposefully not blinking.

Louder, she hollered with angry glare, "Midnight! WHERE'S MY SHOE?!"

Despite the volume, the dog did not seem to notice, kept up its happy wiggling, but Dr. Corgi was instantly afraid.

"MIDNIGHT, IT'S RIGHT HERE, MY SHOE! WHERE'S. MY. SHOE!"

All the other rooms with nice people and pets who were all waiting inadvertently had to tune in to this frightening spectacle.

Dr. Corgi stared. Ms. Brittany stared at her pet with her wide eyes, so serious.

Dr. Corgi's internal thought: *I need to call animal control on this woman! This person has turned mad! Pet abuse in an exam room!*

Ms. Brittany got closer to the dog with shoe. Dr. Corgi instinctively leaned over the dog to protect it. She took both her arms and wrapped them around the pet with the vet assistant, who was also puzzled and afraid. For sure, Ms. Brittany was going after her pet. The Croc swirled over the pet's head, vet, and vet assistant, ready to whack. Midnight now began licking both faces next to her.

This woman is crazy! Ahhh, I need to say something before she is beating the pet through an exam! My exam!

"Ms. Brittany, what are you doing?" Dr. Corgi defiantly stated, cringing, eyes closed, halfway expecting to get beaten by a Croc.

"Well, I'm trying to get her attention," she said sweetly, calmly, suddenly shifting back into the poised person Dr. Corgi knew better. Before Dr. Corgi could leave the state of shock she was in, Ms. Brittany roared again.

"Midnight, WHERE'S MY SHOE?!"

Dr. Corgi peeked out from her hover-with-the-pet stance. "With your shoe...ma'am?"

"Oh yeah, we play this game at home. After I say, 'Where's my shoe,' I throw it, and she chases it." Ms. Brittany smiled pleasantly.

Oh well, okay. Everybody took a deep breath, stood up, and relaxed. Ms. Brittany stepped back. Then Midnight sat for a moment too. Dr. Corgi looked in her ears. They were better.

The staff had to casually explain the owner's "game" to the other clients in the exam rooms and the waiting room. They were all very concerned.

Dr. Corgi to this day will occasionally be presented a puppy overwhelmed in excitement. Trying to ease the inability of being able to get a task performed, she will pour out a stream of sweet Southern coos, trying to get it to calm down. But when the pet's excitement intensifies, Dr. Corgi widens her eyes and, using a possessed-zombie voice, adds in, "Puppy, WHERE'S MY SHOE?"

And her staff giggles.

The Ottoman

Success is stumbling from failure to failure
with no loss of enthusiasm.

—Winston Churchill

I think I was in my fifth or sixth year of small-animal practice. I had left the equine world due to family constraints and military deployments, and I was happy with the decision. I found much satisfaction in making all the puppies and kitties, or anything else small with fur that presented for that matter, better.

I would be presented one of the most astronomically challenging cases due to all the forces that were at work against it. Only about 5 percent did I have control over, but it would leave me in the most awkward predicament. This was one of the most stressful fixes I have ever been in.

In this case, I was presented a dog that looked like a small round table, or maybe a cushy ottoman with legs. Yes, that's it exactly. A plush cushy ottoman with stick legs. It was underneath the most enormous back-fat pad I have ever seen, on a pug. Now, most pugs weigh between fifteen and twenty-five pounds, but some may fall outside of that range. A thirty-pound pug is an overweight pug. "Charles," my small round table pug, weighed in at fifty-five pounds. He was beyond massively obese.

I wish he had presented to me for a routine exam or vaccine. Looking back through his record, I could see the countless times other vets had tried to reason with the owner about the weight problem, but alas, he grew with each passing year. On the other hand, I don't know if I could've offered enough education if I had been the vet to offset the series of events that followed. Charles did not present to me for a routine visit. He came in with a big problem.

His owner, Ms. Eleanor Ridgeback, was eighty-five years old and didn't speak or hear very well. She also was not particularly friendly. She could not drive herself or medicate herself, but she would tell you she loved her pet; he was her best friend. Despite some caring relatives and a nice caretaker, she would say Charles was her ONLY friend. I had never met either of these two until this presentation of Charles.

So how was Charles presented to me?

He was presented in an emergency. Recumbent, lying on the exam table, panting with an open mouth, unable to walk, and he had vomited a few times.

Ms. Eleanor, obviously stressed, fussed right at me. "Something's wrong with him. You better figure it out!"

I had just walked in the room, and I immediately started my exam. Ms. Ridgeback's caretaker, Cindy, was in the room and shaking her head as if to say, "Sorry," in advance of the crass greeting.

Charles lay on the table, his heart racing at about two hundred beats per minute. He was panting, with pink gums which are the best. Blue gums are a sign of lack of oxygen. His eyes were dancing back and forth. This is a symptom of brain swelling, called nystagmus. Nystagmus is where there is pressure on the optic nerve and it makes the eyes dance back and forth. It can be very nauseating. His breathing was labored, and Charles had the traditional pug breathing sounds—intense wind sucking through a compromised airway—that make all people, even vets, uneasy. He lay there, occasionally letting out a confused cry that sounded much like a hoarse caw from a raven or something. Altogether, it looked awful.

There are multiple causes for nystagmus, including nervous system problems like vestibular disease, or an inner ear infection.

Since I didn't have an MRI or CT scanner right there in the exam room, I decided to look into the parts that I could control. After looking at his cardiovascular system and feeling his abdomen, I decided to try to look in his ears.

But where were his ears?

I pushed around in the many folds around his face, trying not to distress him too much. Finally, I had to push an epic mountain of back fat backward, and that's when I saw it—an ear tip. It had been completely covered in, of all things, obesity. I tried to put my ear scope in it. It was pitifully narrow and squashed by fat, but besides that, the ear canal was swollen, ulcerated and filled with green pus.

I said, "Oh my, I think he has an ear infection."

Ms. Ridgeback was instantly enraged by this. "Now he has had many an ear infection, and it never looks like this, so don't you tell me that! I know that something bad is wrong, don't tell me it's his ear, dumb vet!" She proceeded to shake her head in disapproval.

I tried to advance my scope a little into the ear and speak at the same time.

"Well, ma'am, sometimes they get so bad that they cause the animal to look like this."

And with that, my cone tip broke away from my otoscope and bounced off the floor. I caught the cone tip right away. I was going to try to calmly explain more, and I thought about how to approach my next description, but Ms. Ridgeback stopped my line of thinking.

Ms. Ridgeback eyed my ear cone catching with contempt.

"Well, ain't you gonna get a new one [cone tip]? Dog has enough problems as it is."

Oh my, I was never gonna do any good at this point. I still had not approached the weight issue, which *had* to happen. Really, but clearly, it was going to be a challenging conversation, not well received. In addition, it appeared to be largely the main source of this dog's problems.

I said I was not sure if it was only the ear infection or not, but I was worried about his high heartrate and labored breathing, and I asked permission to take him back and give him some oxygen via a mask and do an ECG while I try to get a better Idea.

She agreed. Or at least she gave me an accepting and annoyed wave that said, *"Go ahead...stupid vet."*

I went to the back. My entire staff gasped as they saw this horribly obese pug. I quickly put him on the treatment table because I was out of breath from carrying him.

"What's wrong with him?" they all asked at once, then all added, "Besides, uh, fat."

"Well, I think he has inner ear disease, and its causing nausea and nystagmus. I think the excitement and stress, plus massive fat, are causing the dog's heartrate to be high, but I am not 100 percent sure. Let's get him on some oxygen and hook him up to the monitors."

As we hooked him up and blew him some oxygen, he appeared a little better. We tried to keep him calm and still. We gently swabbed his largely hidden ears to run the test for ear infections.

I looked at the staff. "I have to go tell this eighty-five-year-old woman that I think obesity is the culprit for most of this. His fat obstructed his ear canals and caused the ear infection to become worse. I also think his main cardiac problem is just that, well, he's fat."

Charles was super fat and was a Brachycephalic breed. Brachycephalic breeds have the smooshed-in nose that makes breathing challenging anyway. So, conclusion: yes, a super horrible combination.

I got together an estimate for X-rays of skull and chest. My staff told me that the ear swab was primarily a bacterial infection. Charles needed in-depth ear care with special ointment, a specialized flush, and antibiotic pills. Great. That requires a lot of owner compliance and hands-on treatment for weeks.

Sigh. I did not have a great owner for that. You just cannot control what comes in the door.

I slowly went back in the room. Ms. Ridgeback was sitting, and her caretaker looked worried. She was on a cell phone talking to a distant family member. Ms. Ridgeback was taking deep breaths.

I became instantly worried "What's wrong?!"

The nice woman said, "I think she is having a panic attack, but I need to have her checked out. I'm just going to run her up the road to the ER that's just a block away."

"Oh my gosh! Okay!" I said.

Ms. Ridgeback got up with her caretaker holding her arm, and they went out the door. Her caretaker glanced back at me and said, "Do whatever you can for that dog. He's her companion, and I'm seriously worried about if something goes wrong with the dog." She leaned back toward me and whispered, "That might also do in Ms. Ridgeback."

Oh my gosh. No pressure.

I was not laughing but was tremendously stressed. I had to make the dog well so the owner would live through the ordeal.

Call a canine lipo-surgeon? No, just kidding, Well maybe, not really.

I took X-rays of the heart and lungs. With an ECG and blood pressure reading, I consulted with an internist, who told me she believed he was just fat. Well, that's good, still a big problem though. A problem likely caused by the owner.

I followed recommended treatments for bacterial infections in ears. We started him on flushes and ointments given via the staff. I also gave him some injections of antibiotics and anti-inflammatories to hopefully speed up his healing process. His blood work was okay. The X-rays of his skull revealed a horribly inflamed inner ear canal on both sides.

Charles sat quietly in his kennel for most of that day. His nystagmus appeared to be resolving some, or at least slowing down to almost barely noticeable. I received a phone call from the caretaker later in the day. Ms. Ridgeback was okay; the ER was going to keep her and watch her overnight. "How is Charles?" she asked.

"Well, he's better, but I don't know if sending him home with you is best, given your circumstances. Can you take him up the road? To the vet emergency clinic? Let them monitor him overnight? And then bring him back to me tomorrow? Plus, how do you feel about daily ear care—is that manageable for you?"

At 5:00 p.m., a distant relative of the family showed up, and Charles, now improved some, could walk out through the lobby and out the door with only a mild head tilt. although the head tilt probably could only be picked out by me and only if you were standing directly in front of him. Everyone else just noticed the crazy-looking ottoman-like creature with four stick legs and horrible wind-sucking breathing that could be heard as he walked.

The next day, I reviewed the faxed report from the vet ER. The overnight staff had taken good care of him but indicated a desperate concern for his weight.

Yes.

Charles walked into the clinic the next day with the distant-relative-type person, who left him for all-day monitoring.

His heart rate was better, 160–180, not great, but better. He had very mild nystagmus, but it was almost gone. He seemed happier. He ate some LOW-fat dog food made for upset tummies. He was a nice puppy.

We cleaned his ears again and gave him his ear treatments. We even managed to trim his nails, which had looked like raven's claws.

The caretaker called again and said Ms. Ridgeback was desperate to see him. She had spent the night in the human ER and had fretted nonstop about her pet. The caretaker indicated the vet ER staff tried to talk about his weight as a concerning factor to the family.

Yes, I said, I think I really need to make my point on that. I told her that I felt that it was the root cause for all his smaller problems becoming horrible problems.

"Well," said the caretaker, "Ms. Ridgeback will probably not do a diet. She never does, even in the past when vets have said something to her. She just ignores them with a smile. She is very stubborn. We've come home from a vet visit and she's told Charles to ignore those mean vets and handed him a chocolate donut."

Hmm, yes.

I would have to talk to Ms. Ridgeback. Ugh. She might bite me. I don't particularly care for these types of interventions. However, if this dog gets any heavier, he could die, which would put Ms. Ridgeback at risk too. This is horrible pressure to be under!

I am only used to worrying about the lives of the pets.

For the record, I am a compassionate person, and I hate confrontations. Not all people are like this, but I am. Knowing I would have to have a bit of a showdown with an eighty-five-year-old crass, opinionated lady who is in fragile health was not something I handled very well—mentally. I like the elderly, I have worked hard for them over the years. I always imagine someone helping my grandparents when I manage those cases. This task was going to be exceptionally challenging. I do care and want to be sweet, but I feared, or knew, I would just get ignored. On that topic, I could not be ignored. This person *has* to put the dog on a diet (HAS to.)

In the room, I went without Charles to talk to Ms. Ridgeback. It started in my usual: June B. French, DVM, client communication, which is sweet and cordial and, in this case loud, to help with hearing trouble.

"Hello, Ms. Ridgeback, so glad you are doing better. I just wanted to tell you about why I think Charles got to the stage that he did. One part, it was an ear infection that got out of control, and secondly, his weight is much too high."

"What dear?" She smiled like she didn't hear me. The caretaker chuckled under her breath.

"Well, I know that your relatives are going to help you with his ear care, but his weight needs to go down, or he will continue to have complications."

"What did you say? Weight? I don't understand," Ms. Ridgeback smiled at me.

Was this woman playing me, at eighty-five years old? Counsel to self: must assume all elderly are sweet, endearing people; there is no other position.

Ms. Ridgeback added, "What's high about his weight? I don't understand you, dearie, using all that vet talk."

Well—*sigh*—and then in an uncharacteristically firm tone, I said, "Ma'am, he's fat. He's really FAT. He's so very OBESE, and it is bad."

"Oh well, he's a bit chubby, but at least he's happy, dear."

(Insert LONG TALK ABOUT WHY BEING OVERWEIGHT IS BAD FOR CHARLES. EARS THAT ARE HARD TO FIND DUE TO FAT ROLLS—THIS CAUSED AN EAR INFECTION TO BECOME SEVERE. CAUSED A HORRIBLE NEUROLOGIC EVENT. DOG IS OBESE, fatter than FAT, blah-blah-blah, DOG CANNOT BREATHE WHEN STRESSED, AND ONE DAY SOON, IT MAY CAUSE HIM TO DIE.)

"Well, I just can't put him on a diet. He'll think I'm mad at him."

Me, again, "He is obese, and it is a cause for all of his problems."
Then I added, "Plus, I have a special diet that works great, and the
animals are happy on it."

Ms. Ridgeback insisted, "No, dear, that's a horrible idea, he'll
be so upset."

Upset? Readers, remaining poised is what I do and what you
should do, especially to help the elderly; but let's just recall that yesterday, Charles was screaming with a horrible bird caw, his brain
was swollen, he was vomiting, and he could not walk. But we must
trudge on in this discussion with tact and kindness, or this woman
will bark and reject you, and then you failed. This was, in my experience, the ultimate test in client communication and compliance, and
I was still batting ZERO.

Challenge: I had to dig deeper into my nonconfrontational personality, had to get this person to recognize. Grrr.

Ms. Ridgeback was still talking.

"I just can't put him on a diet. Nope, he'll think I'm mad at
him. I don't want him to think I'm mad at him because, well, he's my
best friend."

Forget sweetness, go for direct.

**Me: "He will die soon from you giving him treats and table
food."**

Then there was a pause.

"Oh well, I guess when you put it like that, I guess I could try
putting him on a diet if you say so."

The caretaker smiled in shock.

HURRAY! MAJOR BREAKTHROUGH!

"But if he looks depressed, I am going to give him a treat
ANYWAY."

Sigh.

With much help from the caretaker and family, Charles got better and, by some miracle, slimmer.

The Plasma Torch

D r. Melissa Braford was at the clinic and was scheduled to do some farm calls one day when the front desk received an emergency call for a horse caught in some metal. Dr. Melissa rearranged her schedule for the day. She asked her receptionist about the call.

"These folks just said that the horse was stuck in some metal and they needed help." Then she added, "They gave me this address. I dunno anyone out that way."

Dr. Melissa Braford checked her supplies in her vet truck and ran through a checklist in her mind. She had sedation, suturing material, local anesthesia injectables, bandaging material, antibiotics, etc. She even double-checked that her wire-fence-cutting tool was on her truck. It was. If there was an animal caught in metal, it was most likely a barbed wire fence problem. When she felt she had everything, she headed out to the caller's address. This client was a new client.

She pulled down the dirt road of the address. There was only one mailbox. The area was heavily wooded. The dirt road led to a metal cattle gate. There was a rough hand-painted sign that said, "Parts for sale."

She stopped her truck and looked at her location. It was a large junkyard of cars deep in the back woods, with an aging chain-link fence running around it. She saw no barn or horse.

Two men walked up to the gate, apparently a son and his father. The son was in his thirties and the father was over sixty, and both were wearing denim that had seen better days. They smiled kindly, but most of their teeth were gone, especially on the father.

The father greeted Dr. Melissa Braford, "Hey there, lady, you the vet?"

"Well yes, sir. Hear you got a horse in trouble."

"Sure do, got something to cut metal?"

NATALIE GRIFFIN, D.V.M.

"Excuse me, sir?"

"Well, he's caught in a car, and we can't figure out how to get 'im or fix 'im."

Dr. Melissa Braford thought about this man's statement. Confusion and subtle concern set in.

"Well, maybe, could I see the horse?"

"Oh yeah, sure. He's in the woods behind that trailer, he's not used to people."

They opened the gate and let her pull into the junkyard.

"How old is he?"

"About two years old, not halter broke yet."

Ugh.

"Where is your stable?"

"Oh, he just kinda runs around the yard here."

Dr. Melissa Braford pulled her truck where he pointed. There were worn-out cars, dismantled and rusted, at every location. There were car parts absolutely everywhere. Not ideal for a horse or dog, or even a squirrel.

She pulled behind the old house trailer, and there, in a cluster of pine trees, was a horse. A young bay colt, his ears perked forward when he saw the people walking toward him. He timidly attempted to jump back, but a loud clang could be heard as something hit one of the trees. A jolt of stress and shock shot through the horse, and he stilled then dropped his head in defeat and fatigue.

As Dr. Melissa Braford got closer, she saw that surrounding his right foreleg was a giant mountain of pine needles. Underneath the pine needles lay an enormous car part approximately six feet long and two to three feet wide. It had acted like a shovel to the fallen pine needles. This horse had stepped in a hole in this car piece and could not get it off from around his hoof. Dr. Melissa could not fully see the extent of how big the car body part was, but the horse's leg was clearly bloody and swollen.

She asked how long the horse had been like that.

"Well, I heard him, whinnying like that during the night, I reckon, probably all night. I called my buddies, they said call a vet, so that's what I did. Never needed a vet before."

The horse stood there and gave another whinny. Dr. Melissa asked about a halter, and luckily, these folks had one, although, they had only put it on him a few times before. She gently walked over, with care and skill for a frightened creature, slipped it gently on with no trouble. As she finished this bit, she noticed a few more locals had shown up and were watching her.

The older man stepped forward.

"You do have something to cut the metal, right?"

Melissa responded, "Uh no, I just have medication and..."

"You don't have a metal cutter!" He looked dismayed and dumbfounded. "Well, why not?!"

"Well, I have a fence tool for barbed wire, but it won't cut a car body part," she stated calmly.

"You're kiddin' me. I can't believe you're a vet and you don't have a plasma torch or something! Surely, you got one on that big truck."

She did not know what to say to this but did recall that this person does not ever call on veterinarians. Despite that, he apparently had strong opinions on what supplies should be in her vet truck.

"Well, sir, we almost never need such a thing. Usually just people who work on metal need that."

"Ain't you ever seen an animal stuck in a car before?"

"No, sir."

"You're kiddin'. Well, how you gonna get him out?"

"Do you have a friend who has something like that? Like a mechanic or something, like someone who works on cars?"

Mr. Junkyard Man groaned and spat on the ground.

"No, well, let me ask my neighbors there." He walked over to his pals, and they chatted. Thankfully, one piped up. He said, "Jim Catahoula has one. He does body repair." No one had his phone number, but his shop was two miles away. So, then, two folks left in a truck.

They came back twenty minutes later with a second truck behind them—a tow truck. The tow truck was new with a nicely painted logo on the side. The driver pulled over to the horse and got out with a case. A big fella, not sure about all this, he glanced around, nodded at the lineup of folks, which had now increased to about fifteen people.

This man, Jim, shook hands with Dr. Melissa Braford, just as the older owner piped up from among the crowd and hollered, "She doesn't have a plasma torch."

Jim, a good man of sound mind, looked at Dr. Melissa and whispered, "Why would you need one?" He shook his head in disapproval of the situation.

Thankful for someone who could see through her craziness, she whispered back, "I generally don't recommend horses be kept in junkyards."

Jim smirked and nodded his head.

They walked over to the horse and formulated a plan.

Dr. Melissa heavily sedated the colt, whose head hung low. They removed as many pine needles from the metal car part as they could. The hoof had gone through a large hole, and they could not get it back out the way it had gone in; but luckily, there were a few inches that separated the leg from the side of the metal. Dr. Melissa wet the horse's leg in hopes nothing would catch fire, she kept dampened wraps around the horse to protect its skin.

With that all in place, Jim began his part. The crowd had now increased to twenty bystanders. Jim, with personal safety gear on, lit up his acetylene metal-cutting torch and put it to work on the three-foot car-body part. With hands as steady as a surgeon and a patient who was happily enjoying his sedation, Jim worked through the metal. With care, he cut two inches away and bent the metal apart.

And then, with great relief, the horse was freed from his metal shackle. The crowd cheered. Jim and Dr. Melissa Braford were very pleased.

Jim handed a bill to the owner, climbed back into his big tow truck with his special tool, and waved good-bye.

Dr. Melissa treated the leg with care and bandaging. Surprisingly, no tendon damage. She went over care with owners and showed them how to change bandages, apply wound cream, and give antibiotics and anti-inflammatory medication to the horse.

Older owner said, "Well, Doc, you gonna get you a metal torch now?"

"No, sir, probably not, but I do recommend a separate area for your horse, maybe his own pasture, fenced, with no metal in the area. Then I won't need one," Dr. Melissa stated.

"Hmm, maybe I'll do that."

Unforeseen Personal Information

U PI is a new term that I need to explain. It involves room conversations. But before I describe it, I would like to mention it does not include the many conversations I have been privileged to share with folks in deep struggles. Stories of cancer, heart failure, and lung transplant. My heart often would break for them. I have adjusted treatments and medications because an owner is on blood thinner or chemo and cannot be bitten or injured while medicating their pet. I have met children with leukemia and cried after I left the room. They were more interested in their pet than themselves. I have heard the story of widows, and I've consoled mothers and young wives of deployed husbands. I have sadly watched families of divorce, and I've been involved in dog custody situations. I listen, pray, and encourage. I believe it is what God asks me to do in these situations. I feel fortunate and blessed that they share their stories with me.

I have a series of stories that are separate in my mind. In order to accept them as part of my day, I can only laugh and shake my head. They are conversations with owners that I would like to coin UPI, *unforeseen personal information*. They are in part the motivation to write. UPI is a close cousin to the term TMI (too much information). For me, UPI usually catches me off guard. I usually am listening professionally when the most unexpected comments pop out, usually intended in humor. It's not too much information—well, sometimes it is—but I am a medical professional after all. Mostly, it's just an unforeseen event. I have mastered quietly smiling or just giving a courtesy giggle in the presence of a client. However, upon exiting the room, I have allowed my mouth to gape open.

(Especially a conservative, modest Christian girl, like me.)

I once had a client with a husky puppy that was particularly hyperactive and had a lot of behavior and socialization problems.

I asked the client if she had ever tried some Benadryl to try to help settle her dog down. Benadryl is a very safe antihistamine in dogs, and it has a nice mild sedative effect. She said she only gave the dog Benadryl at night, when she and her husband want to blah, blah, blah. I held up my hand to frantically try to stop the conversation. Alas, she continued…with specifics.

UPI.

More recently, I had two eclectic brothers in my exam room. Both brothers were about in their fifties. Brother number one had a relaxed, sandal-resort style, with blond hair and gray mixed in. Brother number two had gelled hair perfectly styled, black button-down shirt, and black hair with a little salt mixed in. They had both moved to my neck of the woods from California; they appeared to be close. They were quite animated about their pets, joking and poking fun at each other's pet-parenting. The first brother expressed dismay that his pup, a male Chihuahua, lifts his leg indoors whenever he goes to his brother's house for pet sitting. The second brother expressed his discontentment with this also. I started to provide my opinion, when the second brother, an avid *Animal Planet* watcher that has led to animal behavior authority, no doubt, piped up and said that he understood animals, and then he explained. The second brother, in an attempt to change the inappropriate elimination habits of his four-legged houseguest, goes out to the Chihuahua's dog house every morning during his stay and proceeds to pee on the doghouse so this particular dog understands who's boss. He smiled and said, "Oh yes, I do. He needs to know that I'm boss." He laughed, and then he added in humor, "Uh-huh, and then I wave at the neighbors while doing so."

The second brother then asked me what I thought.

Speechless. (Unforeseen, but I certainly chuckled.)

"I have no words, only joy that you would tell me this," I smiled and answered.

(Because I love the crazy.)

He smiled and said, "Well, you're welcome."

The following story is one of my favorites.

I was working a clinic part-time with an older vet who graduated vet school in the seventies. His name: Dr. Marty Weimer. He once came out of a room, smiling at me and the staff in bewilderment, shaking his head. He had been in a room with an elderly woman who had specifically requested him to examine her dog. She was an infrequent, very frugal, but longtime client.

"What happened?" I said. He just shook his head.

He then said, he was just trying to get over what that owner just said. This particular boss of mine was always solid and reserved and was never rattled. He had practiced veterinary medicine for decades and had plenty of wisdom when he looked at an animal. Sometimes, he would just know with a glance at the animal, or something the owner said, exactly what was wrong. But on this particular day, he looked a little stunned, and my curiosity was piqued.

The long time kennel helper jokingly asked if the elder lady had been super difficult. "No, she was polite," he said. His eyes were still a bit dazed, but a small smile was forming.

He could see we were all very curious and wanting to know more. Slowly, with a soft-humored calmness, he started to describe what had happened. The owner had been interested in her female dog having one litter of puppies. She said she didn't have money for fancy fertility blood tests but wanted something accurate. She was direct about it. He told her that the best days to breed a dog are between nine and twelve days after you notice she's in heat.

I looked at Dr. Weimer. "Is that it? Why do you look stunned?"

(I have no idea about the validity of the following statement. It was not included at my school, but whatever. Dr. Weimer had been around a while.)

"She asked me for the most specific time she should take her dog to the neighbor's to be bred, and I told her that if you rub the inside of the hind leg and the dog hunches its back, it means she might be close to ovulating."

Apparently, this elder had responded enthusiastically and matter-of-factly, "Oh well, yes. **She's just like me.**"

She's just like me, it would often slip in and out of my brain in intense days full of vet madness, in the midst of the hum of barking dogs, ringing phones, endless complicated situations, and frustrating problems. *She's just like me.* It swirls up in my thoughts, I smile, and then it drifts away back to the depths of my memory.

Also, the ten Amish brothers, the 911 call, the night I was covered in hives, the things I hear, the special people I meet. All concerned for their animals. It's what connects us all.

"Honey, there's a tick on your back."

Oh gosh.

The Mystery Fat Cat

D r. Nina Springer began a mobile practice, visiting her four-legged patients at their homes and giving them wellness care onsite. She had a regular feline patient who had notable changes to his waistline. His name was Max.

Max seemed to be an ordinary, tabby-colored domestic short-haired cat. He was relatively nice and dealt with the usual mild conditions of tartar on his teeth, gingivitis, a flaky coat, and long nails. However, there was one thing that set Max apart from some of our other patients. Max had a propensity to gain weight, slowly and steadily, over the eighteen months they cared for him. In reviewing his previous veterinarian's records, Dr. Springer noticed he had admirably maintained this pattern for all of his eight years. Every single visit, his weight went up between half and one and a half pounds, until he was a very sturdy twenty-one pounds, on a nine-pound frame.

At first, Dr. Springer and her technician lightheartedly joked with Max's owners, Debby and Jim. "He's getting a bit fluffy, guys," she would say.

Robin, the technician, was more forward. "You are KILLING him," she'd say. "Food is not love. You are taking two years off of his life. I hope you like giving injections, because you are going to be chained to this cat every twelve hours for the rest of his short life!" *(She was referring to how often overweight cats get diabetes and have to be poked with insulin every twelve hours.)* "You…"

"Okay, Robin," Dr. Springer laughed nervously. "Let's not get kicked out of the house!"

For the umpteenth time, Dr. Springer and Robin carefully went over Max's diet. Their recommendation: two cans of food, total, per day, and one treat per day. Place food in small amounts around the house to encourage "hunting" of food. Use laser lights or ping-pong balls to stimulate play (although the owners admitted the cat was lazy).

"And are you sure only one of you is feeding Max? You know, sometimes we forget to tell our spouse that…" Dr. Springer said, trying to be empathetic and yet root out a culprit for the weight gain.

"Oh no," said Debby. "I can't stand the smell of cat food so Jim does it."

"And you don't have visitors that give him treats?" asked Robin.

"We don't ever have visitors," said Jim. Strange, but then again, so were Debby and Jim.

"Have you been out of town and had someone else feeding him?" Dr. Springer inquired.

"Never go anywhere."

"And these are the size cans you use?" She motioned to a standard 4.5-ounce can of Friskies.

"Yep."

Clearly they were tiring of these questions. And the vet duo was tired of asking them. Every appointment ended this way, and Debby and Jim always gave the right answers.

Robin's eyes glazed over in frustration. Internally, Dr. Springer wanted to scream.

Dr. Springer decided that today was the day to get to the bottom of this. It was time to try the scare tactic.

"All right then, we need to do even more of a workup than we already have. We've done the blood work, which was normal except for the high triglycerides. Obviously, your cat has some sort of tumor that is growing inside him, causing him to gain weight. Our X-rays didn't show that, so there must be a mass that can only be seen by ultrasound or CT scan. I can schedule that for you at a specialty hospital next week."

Suddenly, both spouses were staring at Dr. Springer, worry on their faces.

"Cancer?" gulped Debby. "Are you sure?"

"No, but I am sure that if you are feeding Max exactly as you have told me, there is something terribly wrong that is causing him to gain weight. He's too young for us to give up and let him explode with fat. There is absolutely, positively no possible way that Max has been able to gain weight at every single appointment over the course of eight years with what you've told me you're feeding him." She began to get angry now. She was sick of wasting her time, although a tiny part of her began to feel guilty for being so harsh. What if there was something really wrong with Max?

As Dr. Springer was speaking, Jim quietly got up and left the room.

Really?

In veterinary medicine, often the men were the ones who usually overfed the pets in the house, and here was the probable guilty party slinking away. Dr. Springer was done with her tirade, but now, there was an uncomfortable silence.

Now what?

Suddenly, Jim reappeared from the master bedroom, struggling under a great weight in his arms. "What about this, honey?" He looked at Deb.

In his arms was a forty-quart, under-the-bed storage container with no lid. Inside, spilling over, were forty quarts of different sizes, shapes, and colors of dry cat food. It was enough to feed a shelter full of cats for a week.

"Oh, that?" Debby said. And she uttered the famous last words:

"That's in case we leave the house and he needs a snack. He never eats that…!"

Social Engagements

N ow as I am writing this, I have been a vet for several years. I am also a military wife and very proud of my husband's service. We have lived in several different states, found friendships, and are pros to experiencing different parts of the country. I have moved five times since marriage, had three kids, and have held licenses to practice veterinary medicine in multiple states. My husband has been able to successfully build his military career. On occasion, we have been able to go to many very exciting events where we dress formally. (I do have a lot of fun dressing up in fancy shoes and gowns. I'm pretty girly like that.)

I have a strong rule that all my close friends know well, although most of them don't really get it. This rule becomes especially strong when I have just moved to a new area and am meeting new friends, being introduced to my husband's coworkers, etc. Before I tell you my rule, I want you to know that I love my career and what I do, and I am proud to be where I am. I worked very hard to get here. It is a great job, and again, I love it.

My rule is, outside of work, never let anyone know you are a veterinarian. I dare you to ask any veterinarian about it: Do you willingly tell people you don't know that you are a veterinarian? No. One hundred percent of the time. I love my family life, I stop there. My new friends usually only know me by my first name, my big Southern smile, and my family, and I love that.

When I was working through college, my first boss, Dr. Maltese, used to vent, especially during the holidays, about how he would get treated at the local social parties. Fleas were what everyone he met wanted to talk about. Fleas. It drove him a bit crazy. Football, politics, food—he would've been super thankful. He was third in his class in vet school and a pretty amazing veterinarian. His wife would actually get mad at him for not being completely cordial about it. Alas, he would get super frustrated and become rude.

On our fourth military tour, we were asked to move to a big city, like one of the biggest in the country. I was so nervous, especially for my kids. We got there, and we signed up to live in military housing where pretty much everyone is an out-of-towner. We all bonded like a bunch of newcomers. It is great like that. My husband had been given orders to his dream job in a commanding officer position. We moved in, got the house unpacked. I was slowly meeting all my new neighbors, but I followed my special rule, of course.

We were two weeks moved in when one of the moms asked me to come and sit with her in her front yard and chat while she filled me in on big city life. I thankfully accepted, and we sat there for a while. I love meeting new people. She told me what to avoid and special times of year where military families get benefits. I asked about doctors and dentists, etc. She looked at me after a while and asked directly, "Well, what about you, did you have a career before all this military and moving? Do you work?"

Oh dear.

It's actually not a common mom-to-mom question. Nonworking moms don't like the question, but working moms don't much care for it either. But I was the latter still. Part-time. I had student loans to pay and all. I slowly responded, "Yes, I work."

"Oh?" she said. "What do you do?"

It was a direct question. I like the question *where* better because I can just say I work at a vet clinic and stop there. I had to be direct. Deep breath. (Readers, you will understand in a moment.)

"I'm a veterinarian."

"Oh, wow. That's really awesome!" I am super proud at this point usually; it's what happens next that always gets me. This mom did not have any pets, just kids. Relief. She just smiled big and said that's neat. Asked me how much I work, where I went to school, etc. It was pleasant enough. I was very thankful.

My husband approached and said a casual hello. This mom, Janice, offered to take me out with six of her girlfriends tonight. She was going to be moving out soon and some of her friends and military wives were going to a nice Italian restaurant that is well known. "Would you like to come?"

"Yes," my husband and I said together. I know that often, it is helpful to make friends if you can. My husband is supportive of this. Fellow military wives often know some of the trials you are dealing when you are in the middle of it. They are some of my closest friends.

I went out to dinner. It was a beautiful Italian restaurant with awards on every wall. The food was fantastic. Everyone was dressed so nice, and we were thoroughly enjoying our conversation. There were four or five other ladies my age and one who was slightly younger, Elle. She was more of a newlywed type.

I remember ordering a fabulous dessert and coffee. I was getting excited for the finer aspects of a big city life. The dessert was set in front of me. It looked beautiful. I carefully picked up my spoon. Janice was talking. Some medical topic had come up. She smiled at everyone and announced that our new friend, June, is actually a veterinarian.

Oh gracious. We're formally dining, right? No awkward comments? I smiled, nodded. Everyone nodded and smiled, and I started to take my first bite of the dessert. But Elle got so excited. "Wow, I have a beagle!"

"Yes, I love beagles. That's great," I responded casually.

Her eyes got wide, a big smile, like she was about explode, and she added, "Oh my gosh, I have to ask you about something."

"Sure," I said. "Happy to help." It's true.

"He has terrible ANAL GLAND problems! They need to be squeezed ALL the time. What's wrong with him? What can I do? Why does that happen?"

The stream of questioning went without a breath in between.

The other ladies who were all eating stopped, forks clanking on dishes. Their eyes popped out, and they stared. I slowly tried to explain.

Anal glands.

The number one topic for me to be asked about after I tell folks I am a veterinarian.

The Noro Virus

This story is famous because of how many times I've told it to pet owners. The norovirus is not a dog virus, it's a human virus. It fills ERs with sick, nauseated folks with gastrointestinal rage. When I was living in military housing in the big city, it would go from family to family in the winter. It was and is a most unwelcome guest. It makes your kids miserable. It can affect everyone in a family, except maybe your princess puppy.

Baggywrinkle is a princess basset hound. She has big fluffy beds; she eats top-of-the-line foods. Her ailments are always treated right away. She gets her teeth cleaned every year at the clinic. She is always up to date on vaccines, heartworm prevention, and flea control. However, if you asked her about her life, she would probably complain about the constant array of prescription diet foods her vet mommy has placed her on due to her battle of the bulge. (I give her canned green beans and carrots to help her out.)

It remains, though, that she really loves food. She can smell through cans and baby food jars due to her super-ultrasensitive nose, common to her breed. She has taken soup cans out of my pantry on numerous occasions and chewed on them till she got a few good holes going. Then she would gloriously lick up the broth from inside. Yes, special talent, that's what it is.

She began to get heavy while my hubby was on deployment, and I had my third baby who would happily eat Cheerios in his highchair and then spill them on the floor for the dog, on purpose. Baggywrinkle was always thrilled by this. Baggywrinkle loves children; she loves what they spill. She loves that there is always a morsel of food on their faces, and she loves when they eat meals, because there is always a prime opportunity for something, anything—even moderately organic is okay—to fall to the floor. Yes, feeding time for

Baggywrinkle and dinnertime for the family are her favorite times of day. When she sees an eighteen-month-old toddler in front of her, she is joyously excited, can't wait to lick that face!

She does have an unfavorable side to this love of food: sometimes she becomes quite disappointed. On the rare occasion our family steps out for dinner, we would usually come home to a pee puddle right at the front door. My husband calls it a retribution "accident," or not an accident, more or less, her expression of dissatisfaction.

Baggywrinkle is very low to ground due to her short stumpy legs, and she usually has a casual, slow gait. She walks very slowly, even when you hope for her to go quicker; but truth is, she can be fast. She has indirectly shown us. Her action can happen in a second and involves a talent like no pet I have ever seen. Her keen habit is stepping on a chair with one incredibly stubby leg, flopping her head on the dinner table, and sticking her giant tongue out as fast as a toad. All this, in order to clean the plate of an unsuspecting kid who went to the bathroom during dinner.

This kind of action is much like a disturbing alarm. Imagine, you are peacefully enjoying your Italian food with your family. Quietly, unnoticeably, someone has slipped away to the restroom. Much like a boat on a calm ocean, casual conversation on the side, and you are taking it in, and then suddenly, out of nowhere, a giant whale-like creature with penguin-like feet, flops its head onto your table (*splat*) and extends an incredibly long tongue into a plate of ziti, clearing it out in one lick. It's too fast to react, so, no, she is actually not slow.

Yes, she has toad talent in the blink of an eye, and she loves dinnertime. My kids are wise to push their plates to the middle of the table if they need to excuse themselves, but she is always there stewing at our feet, hoping we forget. But if you asked her, I am sure she would say it was because of the prescription vet diet food.

One time, I woke up in the middle of the night, and my oldest son was calling for me. He ran to the bathroom and made it just in time to get sick in the toilet. Ugh. It had landed in our home: the norovirus. It had visited all the surrounding families in recent weeks. This son of mine, six, threw up all night long. He seemed better the next day. He tried to eat some toast and drink Pedialyte, but I kept him home from school, of course. I got up and took my middle son, four, to his preschool class. He had a normal temp and ate his breakfast just great. Said he felt great. So, okay, I dropped him off at school, my eighteen-month-old baby and sick six-year-old still looking pitiful in the back seat.

About midmorning, my little guy, the youngest, stopped eating. He usually got a snack at 10:00 a.m., but he wanted nothing, not one Cheerio.

Hmm, that's very strange. I hope it's not...you know.

He was usually always in motion, but not today. I began to get nervous that the norovirus was coming. I screamed "NO! GO AWAY" into social media for my impending storm, but alas, by 11:00 a.m., my littlest boy started vomiting. Poor guy had no control, being so young, and eventually, I became painted in it. This would carry on through the afternoon.

My oldest was still unable to eat anything, and he had started to acquire problems at the opposite end.

About 1:00 p.m., I got a phone call. Middle son went to gym class right after lunch, and on the way back, he threw up in the hallway. Great. Nurse asked if I could come pick him up.

Sigh.

I felt bad asking anyone for help, because it's like inviting them to come and get acquainted with Mr. Noro, a ridiculously rude and draining houseguest.

I loaded everyone up in the car and went to pick up my poor middle son. Four years old, he looked at me with tears and said, "It happened in the stairwell, Mommy! And it went **drip-drip-drip** down the stairs afterwards." He cried and looked at me with his big sweet eyes and repeated, "**Drip-drip- drip** down the stairs, Mommy, and everyone saw!"

Poor kid, probably shouldn't have taken him to school. Mommy fail. Oh well, lesson learned, let's go home.

Back to the house. The battle raged on: three kids now very sick. I made myself dinner, did my normal cooking routine, but I noticed as I was cooking that none of the food seemed appealing. It all looked yucky; I didn't even feel like eating cookies, which is very rare. We all sat at the table. Everybody had their drink of Pedialyte with them. The kids picked at crackers and soup and bananas. I stared at my meal, worried about a mommy-versus-noro battle. Very scary to do battle with Mr. Noro in my own body…and be a mommy!

Dinner that night was a meal, but it was a shell of a meal. I am sure Baggywrinkle noticed a slight crinkle in her routine, but she did not seem dismayed.

I called my work and let them know I would not be in the following day. That night, all night, I stayed up with my kids and their violently angry bellies. It was so hard to watch, especially with the little one. Personally, I battled the exhaustion. I kept wondering how many times my kids could throw up on me before the massive quantity of virus dumped on me would actually cause me to succumb to illness. I'm usually so healthy and resilient to these things.

Then about 9:00 a.m. the next day, I had become green with nausea, and my body battle was on. All four of us were on Pedialyte. I kept calling the pediatrician, who kept saying, "Just keep them hydrated."

(Shaking my head.)

Finally, at 4:00 p.m., it stopped; no one had eaten much all day. We just lay there, all of us, like zombies, staring at the TV. I didn't want to move. I was massively exhausted. My friends had offered to help; they kept checking on me, but they didn't get too close. No one wanted to take it home to their house, to their kids. Can't blame them.

Now I had not made lunch or dinner. I just sat on the couch. Everyone had their electrolyte drink and seemed to have fading nausea. Thank goodness. We sat there until 6:00 p.m. It was then that the nonsick family member spoke up.

Baggywrinkle was most distressed; she whined and whimpered at me. I had fed her at 5:00 p.m.—you cannot be late at all; she will tell you all about it. She had loads of water. So I got up to let her out for the third time in two hours. A cloudy frustration plagued my mind.

This pet has no mercy, exhaustion that's where I'm at right now... ugh. She's still whimpering and staring at me, that long, pleading look.

I walked toward the kitchen in a fog and placed a few extra kibbles in her bowl and walked out. She devoured the kibbles and stood in the kitchen door and kept whimpering. Crying, staring at me. Clearly, she was upset; and something that she desperately needed, despite a horrifically ill owner, had to happen right now. The solid walls of her perfect castle were in trouble.

Is there no peace today? Grrr! Forty-eight hours of this noro nastiness, indescribable fatigue, and the dog does not want to let me sit.

I walked back to the kitchen. Baggywrinkles danced about like she was super excited and wanted something. But I had checked every box, dog food, water, potty. I didn't understand.

I shook my head, I stared at her, frustrated that she would not leave me alone, and then I just said with some discontent, "WHAT?"

Long stare. Tail wagging.

"WHAT. DO. YOU. WANT?"

(To which she had an answer.)

She took her long body with stubby legs and trotted over to the stove and barked...at me.

No way, I thought. "Seriously?!"

She barked again and took her nose and pointed to the stove top, which was totally empty. Yes, this really happened. She kept dancing/whimpering about in front of the stove, then again, she did it again—she barked at me and she pointed her long nose up at the stove top...*Get to it...cook.*

I took my hands and began to pretend I was cooking and she danced in approval with her ridiculously short legs.

Yes, that's it, that predinner thing you do. You apparently forgot tonight.

My dog wanted me to cook, because I didn't. Did I mention *princess*?

More Target Practice

I was new to a practice, and I was working one day with a small-animal veterinarian who had been out of school for about a year. Dr. Chartreux was her name. She was poised and proper, with beautiful long black hair. I had been in practice for many years but had only worked here for a week, i.e., I didn't really know anybody. I was trying to have conversations and show that I was knowledgeable and up to date in current therapy, with years of experience. One day, I was asked to express a miniature pinscher's anal glands. I was talking and laughing and telling my stories like I do. This lovely vet was listening and smiling while typing on her computer. She had her back turned to the treatment table.

I squeezed the anal glands. I missed the towel.

(After this incident, I never, EVER let anybody stand behind me during this procedure ever again.)

I shot it all over Dr. Chartreux's back. It was in her long swirly hair. "SORRY!"

She gasped.

She took off her nice white coat and tried to manage the fact that it was in her hair.

I felt like a total dud. What a terrible way to try to make a professional impression. Poor Dr. Chartreux.

(Somehow she did forgive me, I think. We worked together for a long time. She asked me to be a reference for her years later.)

However, just three days later, it happened **again**. It was horrible luck. It did not hit a human this time, *thank goodness*, but it violently sprayed five feet across a top row of cabinets. *Oh sure, great, what next?*

I did not understand; I had been in practice for years by this point. The pet had been moving, and there was a lot of it. I saw it happen (because I was the one squeezing), and it was so bad. It started to drip down the cabinets onto the countertops. Gross, what do I do? I was still recovering from the embarrassment of just a few days ago.

So, I said nothing; the pet holder didn't notice. I told the pet assistant that the pet was done and he could go up front to the owner. I was so humiliated that this kept happening. Why did it not go in the paper towel? *Grrr.*

Now I was in the treatment area by myself. I frantically started wiping down this top row of cabinets. Gravity was my enemy. I got up on the countertops. Wiping, wiping…dripping, dripping… hurry, hurry.

Then I heard Kellyanna, a longtime pet nurse.

"Dr. June, what are you doing?" she asked.

"Oh, just some cleaning! I love to clean!" (*Not true at all*) I kept wiping. This pet nurse just stared at me with a quiet concern.

I know what she was thinking: *The new vet is odd.* I just said nothing.

Luckily, she had noticed me cleaning after I had managed to wipe off most of the evidence.

Yes, well…what do you say? *I really am a lot better than this!?* Ugh.

Hopefully, I could prove over time that I actually had some reliably good qualities.

Eventually, we laughed about it. I finally fessed up months later. I ended up working at the location for years.

I often remind myself that it could have been worse. I once witnessed a vet squeeze and shoot the anal glands contents right up her nose. That poor girl.

Honeybee

T his is a story of what happens to a novice veterinarian who cares a lot and tries really hard but sometimes, it does not go the vet's way. It is a very hard lesson, and it is one that I encourage you to skip over, if you wish to stick to the more fun chapters. I didn't want to include it but felt I should because I believe it gives the daily life of veterinarian trials a very respectful nod. This is Honeybee's story.

I received a call from a farmer forty minutes away. He said he had a horse that couldn't move and had been eating less, or almost nothing, over the past couple of days. I said I would come, and not thinking it was that out of the ordinary, which actually it's not, I headed out. I found the farm and met the farmer, who was probably in his sixties or so. He was kind and concerned. He had a stout frame and big overalls. Glancing around, I had noticed he had some cows. He said he had one horse, and she was in the barn.

That's when I met her. I always walk up to a horse, habit from being a horse-loving kid, to introduce myself to the horse. It is a simple gesture, offering the back side of your hand for a sniff. Despite being ill, this particular horse seemed thankful for the introduction and blew on my fingers and then let me pet her. She appeared to be a cross between a draft horse and an Appaloosa. She had big shoulders and hind quarters and was covered in dapples. She appeared well fed with a grass belly (moderately overweight). She had sweet eyes and friendly mannerisms, like she was meant to be the grandkids' horse. I rubbed her forehead and her muzzle. She leaned into my rub. She seemed very weary. That's when the farmer said, "This is Honeybee." Her name was perfect, and for some reason, I just immediately loved her.

I took her temperature. 104.5—ugh. Normal range is 100–102.5. You could not coax her to move at all. Her physical exam was concerning. She seemed to be in shock, and she would not move her legs. I tried to ask the friendly farmer a bunch of questions about feeding schedules, exposure to other horses, vaccines, etc. Then I hit on it, "Has anyone ridden her recently?" I asked. "Oh, not for three or four days. Jim Bob took her out for several hours four days ago, had her doing sprint work." He shrugged and added, "He wanted to get her going again past day or two I just had figured she was a little sore from that. I mean, he rode her really hard. That's why I thought she was sore."

(Oh no.)

I continued. "When before that ride, had she been ridden? Had she been in training at ALL?"

Mr. Farmer replied, "Oh well, she hadn't been ridden for over a year. She's just been out grazing in a pasture up until that point when he rode her."

I knew what was wrong. A syndrome in horses called azoturia, or tying-up syndrome. Now if you were raised in the pony club world, every little rider is taught that a horse has to be carefully trained and fed. After it's worked or ridden for a set period of time, it has to be cooled back down again. A well-trained little rider knows to avoid tying-up syndrome. This is a severe buildup of lactic acid in muscles that are not used to it. The muscles become damaged severely, overwhelming the body with muscle breakdown products. This man's friend had taken her out and ridden her hard, sprints up hills, no less, **for five hours**. Azoturia can be treated, but this case was severe and advanced, which is terrible for prognosis. I took some blood for tests, gave pain medication, muscle relaxers, and started fluids at the farm. I got the farmer to get her on a trailer (difficult), and he transported her to the clinic.

Back at the clinic, I ran her blood values. Her kidney values were very, very high. I had never seen blood values so high in a horse. I had been trying desperately to read every medical equine book, to consult with every expert equine clinician back at the vet school, to save her. They all tried to help me. I wanted her pain to stop; I wanted her to live.

However, her body had experienced so much damage.

The farmer had a chance to come by the clinic with a "friend" the next day. I spoke with Mr. Farmer briefly. His friend asked me, directly, why she was so sick. I didn't know who he was, but I held back nothing. Deep inside was an upset little pony clubber girl. I explained tying-up syndrome and the cause was that an unfit horse had suddenly been pushed to do a five-hour endurance ride. "Oh, I didn't know that could happen," the friend said. Mr. Farmer smirked at me and nodded his head approvingly. I'm pretty sure, without anyone telling me, that I had just educated Honeybee's sole rider. He just didn't know, and he seemed moderately honest. I have to tell myself that, but it's so hard when you battling the misery of a poor choice.

I poured fluids into Honeybee's IV. I gave her pain therapy and muscle relaxants. I consulted with the equine internists again. She just wanted to go down, she looked so stiff and miserable. I spent over thirty-six hours treating her on the hour. I felt so helpless. I had a lot going on in the clinic with the small animals. There were several that I kept for IV fluids, as a holiday weekend was approaching, and my boss had been out of town all week. I was supposed to leave town in the morning with my husband to go to a planned family event. I had been working with Honeybee during the night and early in the am. I ran inside Saturday morning to meet up with the other doctor, Dr. Quarter. He and I quickly went through all the cases inside—all were small animals. I went over all it. Then I took him out to see Honeybee. She was my biggest concern.

She was down again. I scrambled over to her. I wanted to cry. She was breathing heavily—with each heave she would let out a groan. I could not stand the pain she was in. My heart was breaking for her.

It all seemed so unfair. *Why did someone do this to you? I am so sorry.* My boss looked at her with all his experience and sadly shook his head. I think that besides the horse being in a terrible condition, he could see also that I had been trying desperately to the point that I was overly emotionally involved.

Oh my gosh, I can't leave this case. I have to see it through. She has to make it. I told Dr. Quarter that much. She's too sweet, **she didn't deserve this**.

He looked at me and, with strong diligence, said, "I've got this. I'll get her up. I'll keep flushing the kidneys. You need to go, now go." Staying would've insulted this great mentor of mine. I knew that. My husband just stared, knowing we were already behind schedule (he's used to that, unfortunately), but being a wise one, he said nothing and stared. I leaned over to Honeybee and whispered to her to hang on, it's going to be okay. Then I stroked her neck and rubbed her soft nostril. She snorted back and blinked gently like she appreciated me. My tears crept out to my eyelids and poured down my face. I sobbed over her. I didn't want to leave; the thought made me nauseous.

Honeybee's new doctor helped me up, walked me to my car, and told me to get into the car. My husband quietly drove us off. I had a horrible, sick feeling in my belly. The fine balance of personal life and things you can't help take home with you is often very challenging. For me, it is extremely challenging; and in the world of veterinary medicine, it can be a daily challenge.

Late that evening, I called the clinic. My boss told me she didn't make it. He never could get her back up that day, despite a large effort by the clinic staff; and eventually, he put her down (euthanasia). I still, eighteen years later, cry for her.

Dawn Dish Soap

There I stood pinned against the window surrounded by wild animals.

My main responsibility when I come in to volunteer my time is to perform ultrasounds on a few of the hundreds of pets that come through our local high-volume shelter. Years ago, as part of a grant, the shelter decided to buy an ultrasound, an expensive piece of equipment, and use it for the benefit of shelter animals. Shortly after they purchased it, however, the vet who encouraged them to buy it left the shelter to move on to other pastures. One month later, as God would have it, I signed up, thinking volunteering my skills was something the Lord wanted to me to do, and wouldn't you know, there was a brand-new ultrasound that nobody felt comfortable using.

I get to look at livers, adrenal glands, bladders, and kidneys, just to name a few. It's very exciting and minimally invasive, which I love. Plus, I think the images are fantastic. The heart is my favorite.

On a normal volunteer-at-the-shelter day, I show up to perform about four ultrasounds and go home. I usually have a holder/assistant, and then afterward, I write up my cases. I eventually would become increasingly more involved—being put on a board of directors and going to community meetings, that sort of thing. It is very exciting from a professional standpoint.

One day, I was sitting in the vet office of the shelter when someone ran by me almost in a panic.

"Where is your dawn dish soap?"

Despite a daily staff of about fifty, nobody answered her.

She glanced at me. I smiled and said I didn't know.

She said, "Oh hi, Dr. June, it's okay," and she ran off.

Second person running past me in a panic...

"I need all the Dawn dish soap now! Where is everyone!?"

"I found some over here!" answered another worker. They were everywhere like busy bees in the cabinets and hallways.

"Here, I have three bottles, and there was a gallon of it over by the dog bowl sink. Ugh, it's not enough!"

Now I thought this was odd; many people were fluttering; surely, there was some state of emergency. I just hadn't figured it out yet.

I kept typing my ultrasound notes. I had to get home to pick up my kids off the bus. But note to self: next "Dawn" seeker, ask why.

Then just outside the office where I was sitting, there was a meeting of sorts as they were giving each other a big rundown of how much Dawn dish soap they had collected, and had they checked every location from the shelter, the clinic, the dog bowl area.

I was trying to type, but thinking all this hyperactivity and dish soap was super odd. In veterinary medicine, we use Dawn dish soap to wash off or remove cheap topical flea products from pets. The cheap flea products can sometimes cause seizure-like activity, and washing it off is part of the treatment, but you only need a little Dawn dish soap for one pet in that scenario. However, there is one other use for it that I had not encountered before.

In came the shelter director, Ms. Newfee. "I need all the Toxiban from every clinic in the area!"

"How much?" I asked, perplexed.

She looked over at me, since I am not a regular, and said "Uh, oh. Hi, Dr. June. We've got a situation in Kaytown."

Before I could ask about it, she asked me, "What hospital in town would have a large supply of Toxiban?" (This is the black syrup that we give to animals for toxicity.)

"The emergency clinic probably has a large supply," I responded, confused still. She said, "I need about twenty to thirty bottles." Oh my goodness. One or two bottles are all that sit on a counter for months on a regular vet clinic shelf for the occasional toxic patient.

I looked, puzzled, at Ms. Newfee. "What is going on?"

She seemed distracted and did not answer. Instead, she barked out orders to nearby staff members to call the local vet emergency hospital (which is a fairly large facility) and buy their stock of Toxiban, or as much as they can give.

She looked at me and said, "We've got an oil spill in Kaytown harbor. There are many Canadian geese involved."

"There is another rescue group on the way, but I don't think they know what they're doing." She shook her head at the impending frustration of dealing with multiple animal welfare groups. "We have the experience, we're going." She stared down at me and, in a serious tone said, "There's a lot of birds involved."

Oh.

These folks are so compassionate; this was an emergency, and they were prepared to answer the call. Now, Ms. Newfee, a definite unrelenting CEO type, has an extraordinary amount of both knowledge and sass.

Kaytown is one hour away. Most of the staff members were running for their vans. Because I felt a bit left out of the excitement and uproar, I asked if I was needed. "No," they said. "Dr. Glider and Dr. Bloodhound are coming. Thank you, Dr. June."

"Okay," I said, a bit relieved because I had other commitments.

However, I definitely felt like a kid player sidelined at a fun, yet intense, game.

Eighteen years in medicine and many years being on emergencies, I had never seen such a group effort for animals in crisis. In a way, it was awesome to witness those who care ban together on an urgent mission.

Later, I would learn that the geese were covered in fuel. Dawn dish soap is the safe, gentle, and effective way to remove oils and gas without harming the animal. The Toxiban is given orally to the large birds to try to absorb any fuel that might have been ingested and to safely carry the toxic substance out of their bodies.

When my shelter society showed up, there were a few other animal groups already there, ready to take action. While this seems wonderful, sometimes they do not all play nice. It can be chaotic. In this case, they had a hot debate over who was in charge at the crisis situation. Ms. Newfee, a twenty-two-year veteran to the world of shelter animals, had minimal competition for her wealth of experience and stomped out all other commanding type As at the scene. The first group on scene, since they were nearby, had offered to look after the group of geese at their facility while they recovered. Ms. Newfee did not particularly care for this, and she quizzed them, but then, seeing no alternative but to agree, agreed.

The "save the geese" movement went forward. The birds were bathed, treated, and housed to recover for a week or two at a new facility. Go, rescue folks. Good job.

A week later, I returned to the shelter to recheck a canine patient. Most of the canine patients I need to examine and ultrasound are kept in a large room with about eight dog runs and twenty smaller kennels. There is a door with an open window pane that leads to this room. It is helpful to look through the window to make sure no dogs are loose in the kennel and such.

I must've been lost in thought or something. I do that a lot. I did not look in the window at all. I just walked in.

I suddenly was surrounded by Canadian geese.

They were everywhere, honking at me. There must've been twenty. Recognizing I was not in the appropriate location, I slowly backed away. (Note: I was chased down by a goose as a small child and never fully recovered.)

Oh crap.

I was pinned against the door. I pressed my body along it and slowly tried to sneak out. Twenty pairs of goose eyes stared at me. The geese were blaring their horns, "Why are we here? Who are you?"

I don't know I just need to do an ultrasound. On a dog.

The birds did look to be in good condition. I realized immediately where they probably came from. Meanwhile, someone saw me pinned against the door—my arms, face, and chest smashed against the see-through glass—and quickly helped me out.

Whew.

I looked at my rescuer, Lara, a longtime technician for the shelter and said, "Thanks, they seem ready to go."

"Yes," she laughed.

"They from the gas/oil spill?"

"Yes, Ms. Newfee did not approve of the way they were being cared for at the other facility, so she had us bring them all here."

Oh, okay. Seems about right. I nodded in acknowledgement.

Lara pointed to the main conference room where several large dog runs had been set up and told me that's where I could find my patient.

You have to love a facility that can overcome challenges all while sticking to its high standards of care. All the geese were eventually released in good health.

For the record, I still feel left out; next time, for sure, I will have my gallon of Dawn at the ready.

The Poo Shooter

oard of Directors' Night for phone-a-thon for the shelter. A day I dread all year. Many years ago, the shelter had acquired fifty telethon headsets at a garage sale and managed to have a phone-a-thon every year since to build the medical fund for the shelter animals. It was always a successful fund-raiser; it was just a bit dreadful if you were the one having to be the telemarketer. I really like being a board member. We have to make a lot of big decisions for animals in the community, and I was the only vet. However, once a year, you are required to get on a phone for several hours, calling strangers and raising money. Thankfully, when the folks are local and know you are also a local and helping animals, they are more forgiving. Seldom do I get a hang-up, but once or twice, I have. I had a script I would read and a list of things to do.

This was my third year as a phone-a-thon participant—I let dread fill me early in the day and decided to beg on social media for willing friends to give me their phone numbers and their cash. So much less awkward if I know you are already willing to donate and expecting my call. Please and thank you. I had three or four awesome friends step forward, and then, of course, I would also call of my extended family members, knowing they would listen, not hang up, and be forgiving. Then because they were family, they would say yes (bonus). So, I was ready. Hopefully, the numbers I brought to the shelter would fill up some time on the phone.

During the course of the day, however, I ran into a small dilemma – my youngest boy had a sore throat. For three or four days in a row, he would mention once a day that his throat was a bit scratchy, but he would still be going ninety miles an hour, playing and eating like a champ. He never had a fever. He seemed normal, but Monday morning, he said he thought he should stay home from school, just in case. Not wanting to be outsmarted by my clever seven-year-old, I sent him to school. I told him that, just to be sure, we would swing by the pediatrician's office after school, even though he was way too perky and had no fever.

"Just to be safe, we'll go after school and let her tell us it's just a cold."

He seemed dismayed but got on the bus. As I would later learn, he walked into class that morning, chatty and energetic but super disappointed about not being kept home from school, he announced to his teacher that he in fact had strep throat. She laughed at him, knowing his character. The teacher sent him to the nurse who took his temperature, looked at him, and sent him back to class. At 2:00 p.m., just before school let out, I took him to his doctor's appointment, completely embarrassed that he had gone to school and told everyone that he had strep throat. The nurse came in, took the strep test, and commented that my son was smiley and bright for a sick kid. His doctor looked him over and said the same thing, but then she added, "Let me double check his test. Lately, I have been surprised by who's positive."

Moments passed with her on the computer, then she glanced over at me.

"He's positive."

"What?!" I exclaimed.

"I know, he doesn't look sick."

Ugh, positive, and I sent him to school. Total parent failure.

"Also, he needs to stay home from school for twenty-four hours," she said.

I stared in disbelief at my son, who was beaming from ear to ear. "Woohoo, no school tomorrow, woohoo." He started to dance.

So that night, with my other kids at practices and my husband out of town, I took him with me, to the phone-a-thon.

I met Kitty Mutt at the door. I had already texted my saga. I got points for showing up anyway, but I explained I had some friends to call and I wanted to do my part.

Kitty told me she was going to place me in the office down the hall with a computer that my son could play on while I made calls.

We walked through the crowd of phone-a-thoners busy with their task into a hallway and stopped. Kitty stared at a cage, then looked at me and my son and said, "We just got this bird relinquished today, but I am not sure about him. Tell your son not to touch him." She then move on cautiously, with some distance from the cage, and Michael and I did the same.

I looked at the bird, a little red lorikeet, which is a type of parrot. He watched me. *Hmmm, I wonder what his story is.*

I sat in the office, with a few others phoning in a room nearby, while my son happily played video games on the computer, and I started to make calls. First, my close friend E. K. We chatted for a while. I took down her amount to be donated, rang my noisemaker, and told her how grateful I was. That's when I heard the bell of a fire alarm in the background. "What is that?" said E. K. "I don't know." I paused and listened more carefully. It was not a full-blown fire alarm but the perfect, slow, periodic pitch of a fire alarm with a dying battery. "I think there is just a fire alarm with a dead battery," I told E. K. It was, however, very loud periodically, so E. K. and I decided to end our phone call. I made two more calls to friends. Off and on, I would notice the noise, then it would seem to disappear.

Kitty popped into my secluded phone station, and I proudly told her I had raised $150. She became ecstatic, let out a few whoops and hollers, and, with my donor slips in her hand, started running back through the hall to ring the bell and keep momentum going. As she went through the hall, I heard her yell and then hit the floor.

I peered into the hall. Kitty Mutt was on the floor, crawling away from the cage.

"What's wrong? Are you okay?"

"That bird just shot poo at me!"

"What! Are you sure?"

"Yes! It came out of him with power, horizontal and projectile!"

She sat on the floor, bewildered. "Someone earlier had joked that they thought he was doing it, but I didn't believe them."

We both stared at the bird. The poo had landed halfway across the hall. I stared for a moment.

Then Michael peeped his head around the corner. "Kitty, is there still goodies in that big room?"

"Yes, Michael, you can have some, but watch the bird, he'll get you with his poo!"

Michael, mindful of a poo-shooting bird, got down on all fours and crawled along the floor on the other side of the hallway.

A moment later, Kitty hollered to me, not wanting to venture through, and I watched my kid crawling back through the hallway to avoid being a target, with a bag of M&Ms, smiling extra big.

As I went to start on more phone calls, this time to family, I heard the dying fire alarm sound again. It was coming from the hallway. I glanced in the hallway, wondering if someone might have a 9v battery, it was so annoying and loud. I looked around, no fire alarm seen. I walked about. *Odd.*

I went back to the phones. I was about to call my sister when Michael asked if he could do it. So, I put the headset on his little blond head, and he joyfully asked my sister if she would like to donate to the medical fund for the shelter animals. Being so proud of her nephew, she told him she would gladly donate $30 to the animals. Michael was so proud, he started shaking the noisemaker. He beamed when he saw Kitty, who had ventured through the hallway of fright. "I got the animals $30!" he said. He was so genuinely excited, and I was a proud mommy.

I decided to call my mother, who, of course, was gracious and giving; but in the midst of conversation, we both stopped. A nearby fire alarm bell had gone off full blast. It was ear piercing. We could not talk anymore, and my mother was instantly concerned for me. I said, "It's okay, I am sure it's nothing, but I've got to get off the phone. The alarm seems close by."

"Okay, but call me back and let me know you're okay!"

"Sure, Mom."

I walked into the hallway, and Kitty appeared at the other end as well. The fire alarm stopped.

"What is going on?" I hollered.

"I am not sure. I don't think there is even a fire alarm in this hall." She seemed perplexed. We walked about for several minutes, no fire alarm, and all was quiet.

We stared at the bird in the cage, the poo shooter.

"Could it be him?" she said, looking at me genuinely serious.

"Maybe."

I stared at the bird—crazy. I shook my head.

We went back to our stations. As soon as I sat, I heard a ringing noise like a *rotary phone*. I looked into the hall. There was no one and no random cell phone lying about that I could blame an old-time rotary phone on. There was only one possibility for this noise, and he was red, eyeing me from his cage. I sat back at my desk. I texted my mom that it was a false alarm.

I picked up the phone and dialed the first stranger of the night. I spoke to an amicable lady and offered her my script for requesting funds for the animals. She pleasantly declined, saying she had already donated earlier this year but offered me good luck. Right as she did, the fire alarm went off, again.

"What's that, dear?"

"It's a fire alarm, but we cannot figure out where it is coming from."

"Oh, that's bad, dear!"

"Well, ma'am, I suspect it's the bird in the hallway.'

"What?" she gasped.

"Yes, I am pretty sure."

I took the phone into the hallway with me. The fire alarm stopped.

"It appears to have gone off," I explained. "I really think it's the bird, I just gave it the eye, and he quit." The lady chuckled. I politely ended the phone call, as she wished me good luck again with my phone adventures.

I called another stranger, and as best I could, I asked for money. Before he could respond, the fire alarm went off again. I rushed into the hallway. The fire alarm stopped. I explained to the poor caller that I had a bird who could imitate fire alarms. He laughed. I started to read my pitch, in the background of my talking, I heard the per-

MY CAT ATE ALIENS

fectly timed high-pitched beep of a dying fire alarm. Although very difficult on stress levels, I tried to ignore the startling beeps, since they were not quite as distracting as the full-forced fire alarm sound.

The man actually offered me $20. I think he realized we were the real deal, calling from inside the shelter, which we were. He wished me luck and told me to be safe. The rotary phone rang from the hallway. I peeked out from my desk. The bird stared and ceased any ringing noises. Kitty appeared at the other end of the hallway.

I said, "I know it's that bird!"

She smiled with an acknowledging grin and agreed. She hollered, "Well, do you have any slips with money?"

"Yes, I have one."

"Yeah! We are doing so great tonight!"

She then got down on her hands and knees and crawled past the cage. She was too excited about how well the night was going to worry about a poo-shooting bird. As soon as she made it to the office, the rotary phone ringing began.

"It's the bird."

Kitty chuckled.

The bird switched to the dying fire alarm chirp. I stared at Kitty, shaking my head. In this moment, I became humored by the knowledge that this bird had been surrendered.

"So, did the folks who relinquished the bird happen to mention these attributes?" I asked.

"I am pretty sure they left out that part," Kitty responded, giggling, and added, "He might be a challenging adoption."

"Yes," I agreed. "A bit of a challenge, that one."

Gladly, and to the credit of a very resourceful shelter staff, the red lorikeet did get a home with an exotic collector, who hopefully has helped him learn some new vocals for his talented voice box.

❀ ❀ ❀

Ms. Curl frantically pulled into the parking lot in a sky-blue-and-white '80s Volkswagen van. It pulled in sideways. She stepped out and clearly was wobbly. She had long wavy brown hair that was going in multiple directions and long, unnaturally thin limbs. She had weathered skin, high prominent cheekbones, and a few brown deteriorated teeth. She leaned into her car and pulled Princess Fluff into her arms. The staffers were now all fully aware of the odd call and the most unique presentation of a case *ever*. They met her in the parking lot and ushered her inside the clinic.

She looked at Kitty and said the vomited alien baby was in a plastic sandwich bag in her pocket. Her breath almost knocked Kitty over.

Kitty got her into an exam room with Princess Fluff. Princess Fluff looked well, but Ms. Curl did not. She seemed so pale.

Then Ms. Curl pulled the bag with its now-infamous contents out of her pocket and set it on the table.

And there it was: a huge hairball.

Dr. Bloodhound came in, carefully examined the slimy wad of hair, and confirmed it to be, in fact, a hairball. Ms. Curl fainted.

My Rescue

We make a living by what we get but we
make a life by what we give.

—Winston Churchill

I was standing behind a stage at a gala when I noticed her. The board of directors members for the rescue shelter had to go out on a stage and exhibit a shelter animal and talk to a news reporter about each one. I was waiting my turn, with a puppy in hand and dressed in a formal gown—an odd mixture.

I love the brachycephalic breeds for their fun spirits. Brachycephalic are smooshy-faced dogs, e.g., pugs, Boston terriers, English bulldogs, and such. I noticed this little French bulldog on the stage of an SPCA fund-raising gala being walked around by the owner of a car dealership. The dog appeared to be engorged with huge lactating teats. She was slightly nervous but easily led and paraded for potential contributors. My heart couldn't help but leap out to her. A momma dog, and she was being so good.

A young fellow from the board, who was holding two tiny kittens and a beer, kept trying to talk to me, but I was distracted. *I wonder if the Frenchie is spoken for...*

In 1997, I had found a puppy in the mountains and named him Camper. He was a little copper-colored hound with a white patch on his chest and was one of the best dogs ever. He even successfully completed therapy dog training at age two. He would play dead if you asked him if he would like to be a fan of our rival university. He died in 2007 from a vicious cancer called tonsillar squamous-cell carcinoma. I was seven months pregnant with my third child. I had a tough time recovering from this loss of my great dog, but we still had

197

our Basset hound, Baggywrinkle. With all the chaos of family life, especially caring for young children and the many military moves, I did not feel taking on another pet. To me, it's like having another child. And I had so much chaos already. So, I waited.

Now, at this point, my youngest son was five years old. I had started to walk around the SPCA and look at all the pets in the adoption area—so many fun faces, too many, but none seemed to stick to me. I decided it was past time to open my doggy door again. Plus, Baggywrinkle was never really a momma's girl; she had always been a daddy's girl.

So there I was at the gala, and this little momma dog had caught my eye. She had just been turned in eight weeks ago with all of her one-week-old puppies. I thought from a distance that she was really old. She was so wasted in her haunches, with big boxy ribs jetting out over an empty abdomen, and she was still giant in her lactation apparatus. The SPCA had been trying to bring her back to health. She also had allergies and ear infections.

The next Monday, I walked into the shelter and went back into the treatment kennels, and there she was again. Lady Bug. I stared at her, and I just knew, like a voice inside me…

That one.

She stared quietly and urgently at me.

Lady Bug had been in foster care because of her puppies. She could not be adopted until her puppies were weaned, and she was about to be spayed. I thought she was too old, perhaps, to be happy in a house with three kids. But I opened her kennel, and she came flying out like a rocket. She jumped all over me with kisses and gave me one hundred French bulldog piggy snorts in my face. That was it, I was sold. Not old or slow. Turns out, she was only five years old and bounding in energy. She was spayed and officially adopted by me. Dr. Bloodhound even fixed her narrow nostrils for me so she could breathe easier, and **bonus**, snore less. (So…she got a nose job during her spay).

She has done well on a hypoallergenic diet, but I sometimes wondered, looking down her horribly scarred ear canals, how many years she had battled allergies and ear infections before someone figured out that she's allergic to chicken, among other things.

Now she roams my house, never more than five feet away. She is always concerned about where I might be, but she has relaxed into a routine. She just wants to be near me if she can, and I love it. She loves to play with my kids. She chases balls with zest. She loves bus stop trips and car rides. She loves all our family's attention. Lady Bug even got Baggywrinkle to play again.

She has a funny habit of always needing to hide behind a bush to go potty. Modest girl.

In addition, she has also taken over as...the backup mommy.

The minute my boys start to wrestle and roughhouse, I can hear her woofing at them. She doesn't like it. It's like someone yelling, "Stop it!" They usually all stop and stare, disappointed; they try to calm her. They know what follows next: me, piping up from upstairs, "What's going on!?"

Every mommy could use a little backup.

I even caught my boys closing the door to their rooms to have wrestling matches. I asked why, and my oldest responded, "So Lady Bug would not bust us wrestling." Silly boys, mommies and momma dogs make a good team.

Once a week, I usually drive the kids to school. It's usually the day after a long day at work and I just want to sleep an extra twenty minutes. Lady Bug rides with us in the lap of my ten-year-old. She is so thrilled for this short car trip, always. After the kids get out, I do the traditional mommy stare watching them all walk into the school at the last minute. One day, I looked back to Lady Bug and I noticed she was sitting up on the booster seat, also watching each of the kids very closely till they disappeared into school.

I just love her.

Frilly

D eep breath. Time to tell this story, for the funny side of it all. Sally says I have to write this story. Just because it's part of it all. This story belongs in Nicefolksville, because that is where it happened. I was in my first six months of veterinary practice. What started out as a personal inconvenience would end up haunting me in embarrassment for my career, so quite the challenge just to write it.

To summarize where I was, I was engaged to be married to Marshall, and my wedding day was very close. It was the year 2000. I was working twelve- to eighteen-hour days and often getting called in after hours. It's hard to take care of personal things at this rate. Marshall did not live with me until after we were married (we are traditional), so I was on my own for the most part, or usually until the weekends.

Just a few weeks before, I had gone down to my university on a free weekend to celebrate with my girlfriends for one last time at my school. It was a small bachelorette party. I had all the usual silly games, with cakes, coffee, and lingerie. Some of the gifts were quite risqué, just to be super funny, and so everyone would get a good laugh. It was just like many other soon-to-be-married parties I had been to for my other girlfriends. Most normal brides have some form of a party like this. It was a good weekend. We had fun.

What does this have to do with anything? I had a broken washer and dryer. I was in the process of getting a "new" used set from a local seller, but I was so busy at the clinic, plus, I did not have a truck that could carry the washer and the dryer. I also did not have anyone to help me load them up from the old fellow I brought them from until the weekend.

This left me in a bit of a pickle. I was very busy, and unfortunately, I was running out of clothes.

I got up one morning, dead tired, but I was supposed to be at work every day at 8:00 a.m. I hurried around my townhouse, trying to get ready. I opened up my top drawer, and there were only a couple of options, both of them awful. Yes, they were from the party. I groaned. These types of underwear were not what I was hoping for. Plus, if anyone knew...*Ugh. Super embarrassing.* But I had no choice. It was, like, 7:45 a.m., so I had to just go with it. I grabbed one of these superextravagant personal items. I picked out a solid pair of khaki pants and a long scrub top and told myself it was fine, no one would ever know. I left the house and went to work. I went through my day with no trouble. I made sure at all times, when I bent down or anything, my top was over my hip area, so as not to be too revealing.

Sally said my next patient was a horse with a sore foot. It was out in the stock trailer. Sally gave me long look and asked if I could examine the horse in the trailer. These folks were neighbors of hers, and she said they had a lot of trouble getting this particular horse on and off of the stock trailer. It had been lame for a few days, but they actually they think it's just a hoof problem.

"Do you think you could do an exam with the horse still on the trailer?"

"Oh well, I could try. Maybe it is just a hoof problem," I said.

With my mind still on the hoof of this horse, I got a pair of hoof testers out of the equine treatment area. They look like large circular pliers. They are for squeezing the hoof to see exactly where the problem is. Every lameness exam should begin this way; that was what I was taught. I also grabbed the hoof knife while I was at it.

I walked toward the trailer and introduced myself. Mrs. Colby and her son Jack, Sally's neighbors. "Sure, how do you do." Mrs. Colby was a middle-aged woman of about sixty-five. She had silver hair pulled back and a long, cotton muumuu dress on. Jack was her son, about thirty or thirty-five, wearing a flannel shirt, big boots, and jeans. He gave me a Southern nod. They both seemed pretty mellow and cordial.

I walked up into their trailer. We talked at length about the signs and symptoms of this horse. It had become acutely lame after running around a field. The field was very rocky, and they were concerned. The horse was now very lame on its foreleg. I ran my hands down the leg and over the tendons—nothing seemed off. I decided to try to assess with the hoof testers because it sounded like a hoof abscess or a hoof bruise.

I started my hoof exam. I looked to my side as the hoof was sitting between my legs, like the farriers do it. My scrub top was down past my hips. Good. I thought, *I'm okay.* Mrs. Colby and Jack stood behind me at the horse's head, watching me carefully.

I tried to find the spot where this horse's problem was coming from. I seemed to localize it over a part of the hoof that I could tell was a little purple, and there was even a very small hole. I examined my culprit for several minutes. I chipped away at the hole a little with my hoof knife so the hoof abscess could drain a little better.

A bruise, and a small abscess, already draining! Excellent! The treatment should be straightforward. I went after the little hole with the knife a bit more.

I was about to put the hoof down and tell the owner what I'd done when she spoke up. She seemed concerned. In a thick, slow, Southern twang, she said, "Honey, there's a tick on your back."

I instantly panicked.

I put my hand on my back. All the skin of my back was out for all to see. I took my hand and slapped my hip—desperately, hoping it was not true. I felt my pant level at my fingertips; somehow, my pant line had managed to slide to a "low rider" position, a small tick on the bare skin of my hip; and exposed high on both my hips, much to my dismay, was my very-frilly, super-lacey string underwear, complete with a large, centered bow, for everyone to take in.

Mind blank…ultimate fear coming true.

Humiliation crashed over me in an exponential tidal wave.

I stood up, pressed my underwear down, and ripped the tick off. I tried desperately to remain calm.

I said, "Oh well, thank you."

"Uh-huh, sure, dear," said Mrs. Colby, with a gleam in her eye and a smirk on her face.

I hustled out of the stock trailer. I glanced back.

Her son Jack said nothing. He just stared.

I blurted through the treatment protocol for the bruised hoof. "Epsom salt soaks for a week, here's some Bute for pain…blah-blah-blah." I wished the folks good day, said it was nice to meet them, and hoped silently that I would never see them again, *ever*.

I ran into the clinic and vented my pure humiliation to Sally. She laughed uncontrollably. She thought it was the funniest story yet. She would bring it up all the time, when it was just the girls. She said that I was always the professional, and that's why was just so funny. I still think it may be one of her favorites; actually, I know that.

Years later, Sally would tell me that, after that episode, Jack, the co-owner of that horse, had gone around to all the surrounding farms of their countryside trying *really* hard to find another sick animal in need of vet care. He even would offer to take them into our clinic for the owner. He said he would never go anywhere else but to our vet clinic, that it was the best.

Great.

Ms. Curl Awakens from the Alien World

Ms. Curl fainted and fell flat on the floor. A 911 operator already had paramedics on the way. Ms. Curl came to a minute later. Her eyes fluttered, and she asked, "What happened?"

Kitty told her she had passed out.

The ambulance pulled up in the parking lot, and in came two nice fellows who quickly assessed Ms. Curl. The paramedics said she was suffering from low blood sugar; they said that, also, she appeared to have a diet made up more of methamphetamines than food, and she confirmed that. Ms. Curl nodded to the suggestion of a soda and a candy bar. She came back to life some; she did not mention aliens.

A policeman who showed up took a serious look at Ms. Curl and offered to drive her home. She accepted. Everyone sighed relief. Everyone was thankful, even if she didn't pay for any of the services.

Kitty shook her head and smiled. Never a dull day.

I gotta tell this one to Dr. June. She loves a crazy story.

(Continued from beginning of book)

Back to the saga of "the shelter dilemmas."

I sat there pondering in the dark of the ultrasound room, and asked God what I should do. How can I reward the shelter workers for their unyielding compassion? Making an annual, $10,000 donation was not in my means. How else could I help the shelter? I wondered.

What could I offer, besides my skills at ultrasound, beyond my ability to help a sick animal that could make the shelter money?

Maybe…a collection of outrageous vet stories? I certainly had those in spades. Would people like to read about the inherent craziness of animal medicine? Could a book like that help a shelter, somehow?

Maybe. Maybe, but that would be so crazy.

Several months went by.

Squeaks, the shelter Pomeranian, formerly owned by an animal hoarder, had made it through her heartworm treatment. Her recovery was a miracle. Upon her initial ultrasound, I had found no evidence of a worm in her liver vessel, so not a grade 4 heartworm disease, I had decided (*although I didn't look very hard, for fear I would find one*).

I knew Squeaks had a chance because I had once seen a jaundiced beagle survive the most advance level of Heartworm disease, grade 4 of 4 with treatment, and she went on to do well. I decided to recommend Squeaks for treatment that day instead of humane euthanasia. Shelly smiled and volunteered to foster the Pomeranian. The clinic approached treatment with small, cautious steps, killing the youngest worms first.

Two months after beginning treatment, Squeaks presented with lethargy. Shelly had noticed that she was much sleepier than usual and that her urine had an odd color. We performed a second ultrasound. There was a consistent hint of a worm fragment in her liver. Her kidneys had poor to no blood flow, and she seemed pale. She had unfortunately progressed to a grade 4 heartworm disease, a condition also known as Caval syndrome.

Despite this, we opted to continue treatment. We injected an arsenic compound, Melarsomine, into the lower back muscles. We were desperate to save Squeaks. The heartworms were actively killing her, and we ALL loved her. We just could not give up.

Shelly saw Squeaks through her difficult treatment, which became a tumultuous road for many weeks. Her coughing in the initial phase of treatment became very severe. The veterinarians poured medications into her to help her. And, against the odds, **she lived**.

And Shelly adopted her.

Squeaks and Shelly became the best of buds. They became totally inseparable. Now, Squeaks has her own Facebook page (and I am a fan).

Soon thereafter, the clinic received a $10,000 from an unexpected source, a large company looking to donate. (Amen.) It seemed the clinic and the shelter were adequately funded. The threats by the longtime donor asking for inappropriate favors were not going to affect them.

By this point, I had already begun to act, or rather *to write*, trusting God and this crazy idea of mine. Would a book of crazy vet tales do well? Could it, perhaps, provide help to a shelter?

I hope so.

In the midst of writing, I happened to catch an interview with Joan Rivers. She enthusiastically quoted Winston Churchill. The quote she used incredibly encompassed my attitude toward my crazy stories on a difficult day. Often veterinary practices deal with a difficult trial in our line of daily work, compassion fatigue.

The quote: *"Make someone laugh, and you give them a short vacation"* (Winston Churchill).

In God's perfect timing and more to the purpose of this book, I also found this Churchill jewel:

"A pessimist sees the difficulty in every opportunity; an optimist sees the opportunity in every difficulty."

And I think I will choose the latter, choose to be an optimist. It can be very challenging. Amidst all the craziness of animal medicine, amidst all the funny stories, there is much heartbreak as well.

We live for the opportunities to help, in whatever ways we can. The compassion for animals drives us, the animal workers, to continue to hope for the miracles.

Which brings me to my final thought:

Can I do this?

"I can do all things in Christ who strengthens me" (Phil. 4:13).

Digressions

I used to tell myself, when I ran into these situations where I had an initial meeting and you could see the lack of confidence all over the face of the client, because I was young and different from the norm—this saying I told myself again and again, because my confidence could be wrecked often: **"All you can do is the best you can do."** It motivated me to always try hard, even if you got hard looks or the diagnosis was unclear. Often, I said it in the middle of the night, or in an emergency, where I just wished I had all the pleasantries of my vet school days back: someone to hold the animal for you, a professor down the hall to tell you you're on the right track, a pharmacy full of every supply, a lab to run all of your tests. I had one professor, Dr. Paca, who was real and who taught us often, "When you don't have exactly what you need, **improvise and overcome**." More often than not, you are the only hope for that animal. *All you can do is the best you can do...*

And you can pray.

Dear Reader of my Book,

Thank you so much for spending time reading my stories! I hope you enjoyed!

Sincerely,

Natalie Griffin DVM
Follow me on Facebook and Instagram!
(@mycatatealiens)

Thank you to my wonderful contributors!

Emily Peck
Cindy Roberson
Carrie Grace, DVM
Tracy Jagocki, DVM
Scott Richardson, DVM
Michelle Richardson, DVM
Rebecca Fratello, DVM

Special thanks to

D Pugh, DVM, MS, MAg
Dipl ACT, ACVN, & ACVM,
Wendy Seesock

And Allison Genovese, DVM, shelter medical director and dear friend, for informing me of the rarest vet case ever to present to a clinic —a cat who ate aliens.

About the Author

Natalie Griffin, D.V.M. has been practicing veterinary medicine for eighteen years. She currently serves on a board of directors for a high capacity, adoption-focused SPCA. In addition, she also serves on another board for animal welfare for her local community. She currently practices in small animal medicine.

Her husband has enjoyed a military career and is presently active duty. As as result of multiple military moves, Dr. Griffin has had the unique advantage of practicing in seven different states. Her wide variety of experiences includes many various types of veterinary practice, including emergency, equine, mixed animal, small animal, and her special love, shelter medicine. Dr. Griffin is a wife, a mother of four, and an active member of her Christian church.

In her early years, from the time she was five years old, she loved animals, and she wanted to be a veterinarian. She rode horses competitively in shows, events, and pony clubs until she went off to college to pursue her vocational dream.

Currently, she is the proud mommy of two adopted fur babies, a black shepherd and a lively french bulldog.

CPSIA information can be obtained
at www.ICGtesting.com
Printed in the USA
FSHW011156230919